HOW TO KEEP YOUR
MARRIAGE
FROM
SUCKING

HOW TO KEEP YOUR
MARRIAGE
FROM
SUCKING

(THE KEYS TO KEEP YOUR WEDLOCK OUT OF DEADLOCK)

GREG BEHRENDT & AMIIRA RUOTOLA

DIVERSION
BOOKS

Diversion Books
A Division of Diversion Publishing Corp.
443 Park Avenue South, Suite 1004
New York, NY 10016
www.diversionbooks.com

For more information, email info@diversionbooks.com

First Diversion Books edition July 2018.
Hardcover ISBN: 978-1-63576-387-4
eBook ISBN: 978-1-63576-386-7

Printed in the U.S.A.
SDB/1807

1 3 5 7 9 10 8 6 4 2

For the brave, beautiful, and gutsy lovers
that know adversity is no match for true love...
(and that marriage can be really fucking hard).

contents

HOW TO KEEP YOUR
MARRIAGE
FROM
SUCKING

introductions

WE HAVE TRIED TO write this book for the last three years and have failed repeatedly. The first writing of it coincided with a particularly dark period of our marriage where we were on the verge of splitting up and were desperately searching to find the love we had for each other. The second time we tried writing it we were in a much better place as a couple, but then Greg was diagnosed with lymphoma, and we put down the book and concentrated on his treatment and wellness. Thankfully, with the help of some fantastic doctors and surgeons, Greg's health improved, and he became cancer-free. At the time, we didn't think about picking back up on writing this book. It felt like the book just didn't want to be born after that, and so much time had passed already that we just had lost our mojo for it.

But then some of our friends split up. Marriages that we had admired had crumbled and left loved ones dealing with the horrific wreckage, and some truly interesting revelations came to light during those friends' breakups. A few of our friends, once they had some distance from their dissolved marriages, had begun their new lives. Some were dating, some were just dealing with coparenting with their ex, and some had sworn off relationships altogether. But all had done a fair amount of soul searching and had come to interesting realizations.

Two recurring themes brought us back to wanting to write this book. The first was that, had those friends known how hard it was to be single again, they would have tried harder to stay married. The second was that, if they had to do it all over again, they probably would have made the same choice of spouse but just done "it" all differently.

So, the third time being the charm, we dove back into the idea of *How to Keep Your Marriage from Sucking* with the additional approach of wanting to fully understand how our choices in the early years of our relationship trigger long-term behaviors that can be a one-way ticket to Suckville. Starting at the beginning of our relationship, we've worked our way through all the things that have bitten us in the ass as a couple and have made a suggestive road map for you to consider as you build your own hopefully suck-free marriage.

• • • •

GREG'S INTRO

When you pick up a book about marriage, you assume that the author has cracked the code, found the solution, and holds the key to marital bliss. But this is not a "We've done it right so follow our lead" type of book. That would be disingenuous and a little sanctimonious. (By the way, if that book exists, please pass it on.)

My marriage to Amiira has been beautiful, but it has—at times—downright sucked ass. We've made mistakes with money, property, and time. We've spent years not understanding each other while also being celebrated for understanding each other, and we've gone through periods without sex and without work. We've dealt with mental illness, addiction, rage, age, losing family members, and wrinkles, and that was just last week (ba-dum-dum!).

But we've also been very happy, proud, and in love with one another. We have fought demons and sadness side by side, even when we weren't side by side. We've known great joy and laughed probably more than we are supposed to. We've known success that came from our love for one another and success due to our own individual creativity. We've raised two kind, funny, considerate, beautiful girls who seem to like themselves and are the center of our known universe.

This book is not just for people who are already married but for people who are considering it as well. Though we are writing this book as a straight couple, we believe that this book can be appreciated, loved, and/or hated by anyone who's entered into the bonds of terminal togetherness because we are all still humans reacting to each other and having a human experience. We support all marriages—gay, straight, or otherwise—and we are all about you getting the best out of your life.

What this book does is shed some light on what a marriage is or can be. Hopefully, it can help you avoid some of the dark places we've been to, or at least learn to deal with them when they happen. Just know that you are not alone in this thing called marriage.

You've got your person, and you've got us.

• • • •

AMIIRA'S INTRO

It all starts out looking like you're going to beat the odds. You're in love, you're an extension of each other, you're completely in sync, you're the envy of all the (secretly sad) single people you both know, and you're crazy close to your goal weight. You're winning at life and love because life is love, and YOU'RE IN LOVE!! You can't even foresee a time when you might feel differently about your amazing soul mate because they are the perfect match for you. The yin to your yang, the pea to your pod, the lid to your pot, the whatevs to your whatever.

But, hear me loud and clear: That shit will end. I've been you, and it is delicious, this glowing perfection bubble that your love lives in where you like 92-95 percent of your future spouse. It rules. It's this glorious period that etches itself on your heart so that, later, when you can't stand the sight of this person, the nostalgia can kick in to keep you from prematurely divorcing or killing said once-perfect person in their sleep.

I've been married twice, so I'm not the person still holding onto the concept of "'til death do us part" with starry eyes and white knuckles. I ditched out predeath on husband number one, and I can do it again. I can be a quitter if pushed—just try me. I want my marriage to Greg to last. I like my husband, for the most part (most of the time), and we still have a lot of laughs together, which means there's still some of that glowing perfection bubble etched on my heart.

I want to have a home that my children want to come home to for college breaks. I want all of us to be under one roof. I don't want my kids to have to choose between their parents and divide up the holidays or to like their stepmother more than me—that shit will not fly.

So I work hard at staying married. I work hard to try to keep my marriage from sucking because, boy, it can suck sometimes, and that sucks. Really sucks. Monumentally sucks. But my marriage is worth trying to resuscitate, so I crank up the home defibrillator and try to get a pulse back in that bitch. Yes, marriage is a bitch—it's true. That's why it says so on mugs and magnets. Mugs and magnets do not lie. Marriage takes two, though. You can't single-handedly bail water out of the sinking *USS Matrimony*, so luckily my husband also wants to stay married. (And, why wouldn't he? I'm great 43 percent of the time.)

We've been married eighteen years and together for nineteen. That's a hefty fraction of my life that I've invested in this relationship, and I'm one that likes to see a return on my investment. We've had super high highs and super low lows. That's the "for better and for worse" stuff that they talk about (super briefly) when it's nearly too late to change your mind...unless you love a church full of glaring eyes boring through you to your core.

While we haven't experienced everything you might encounter in a marriage, Greg and I have covered a lot of ground, and we are here to share our experiences and report our thoughts on the things that you don't think will matter but matter. We wish you nothing but love and luck as you enter into these first years of marriage. It takes a lot of bravery to stick with something. Quitting is easy, just ask me.

marriage
schmarriage

THERE HAS LONG EXISTED the debate as to why getting married matters—or if it actually does. Love does not need the legality of a marriage for it to be profound, and, yet, millions upon millions upon millions enter into marriage every fifteen minutes. Okay, that might not actually be an accurate statistic, but many people get married each year, more than probably should. We are not of the belief that marriage is a necessity, and don't even for a second think that we've gotten this whole marriage thing "right." Or that we've even managed to do our relationship any more "right" than anyone else. We just happen to have a computer (humblebrag) and have experiences to share.

The thing about us as a couple is that we both believe in marriage and wanted to be married to each other. It mattered to us as it does to so many. Not just for the rights it offers us to care and advocate for each other legally, but for what we think it says to each other about our love for one another. There is no grander gesture that we felt we could take than to try to commit to a lifetime together, since neither one of us was wealthy enough to buy the other an island. Both of our parents had lengthy marriages that taught us a shit ton about resilience, loyalty, love, likes, tolerance, generosity, and the glue that makes family FAMILY.

There is a tradition and a symbolism to marriage that resonated with us. At the end of the day, we are loudly singing the praises of why, when everyone around us fell, we didn't, despite the multiple challenges we faced. We believe in marriage. Otherwise we wouldn't write about it, and this would be a shit book by a couple of self-help opportunists cashing in on a career in self-help. We've been to hell and back three or four times since we first started typing, and it was our marriage that kept us together—not the other way around. Our marriage is the hard-earned equity of nineteen years, two kids, five dogs (not all at once!), surprising success, great losses, bad economy, the internet, cancer, rehab, career changes, sobriety, aging, and writing this book. It is battle scarred and bruised and often too tired to have sex...but it's ours, and it's beautiful. At its core, it is pure, complicated, deep, and eternal love that no one person and no one situation will ever change. Even our occasional hatred of each other is made of love.

People want to naysay the tradition or concept of marriage or get on their soapbox about the patriarchal roots of men having women as property, but that's not what marriage is today. There are those that say that a piece of paper proclaiming itself as a marriage certificate doesn't mean anything—but that's a crock of shit. *(Sidebar: First of all, a piece of paper doesn't proclaim anything, and, if it did, we suspect it would proclaim something like, "Make me into an airplane so that I can fly!")* It's like saying that the Super Bowl is *just* a football game. It is a football game, but it's the most important football game of the year, so let's not pretend that it's *just* a football game—even if you only watch this particular football game for the commercials and halftime show. We don't pretend the life-size Bob's Big Boy statue in the San Fernando Valley means the same thing as the Statue of Liberty, so let's not keep trying to hard sell the idea of a certificate of marriage being meaningless. Or that marriage is meaningless. If it were meaningless, people wouldn't still be doing it or have fought so hard to have the right to do it.

The only parameters that belong on the union of two people are those set by the participants. If the institution of marriage falls into those parameters, then good for you. You're in for something special.

We have always felt that our books work for anyone. Switch a few pronouns around and the basic principles of creating great moments for your partner are still there. While we can only come at the topic honestly from our place in the world, what we advocate is a fit for everyone: knowing your worth and living by a standard where people treat you with the same respect and dignity you show them. Advice and enlightenment aren't limited to gender-specific anything; we all get to enlightenment when it clicks for us personally.

• • •

WHY GET MARRIED?

Here's the honest truth: Being married is the thing that will keep you from walking away when things get too hard. It's far easier to bail on a relationship that isn't bound by law. Remember that piece of paper that some think is so meaningless? Well, any time you have to sign a piece of paper to enter into something, there's a very good chance you have to sign a piece of paper to get out of it. Usually, getting out of something is far more difficult than getting in. There are countless married couples that have told us that the reason their marriage has lasted so long is that neither of them ever wanted a divorce at the same time. Sure, that's a glib answer that's as amusing as it is truthful, but there really is something in that idea that many long-time married couples relate to. (Including ourselves, to be honest.) Part of deciding you want to marry someone is the bravest part of you saying I will legally bind myself to you so that I am forced to work harder and fight harder to keep this love alive, even when things totally fucking suck.

Marriage is a voluntary commitment made from an internal motivation of love and devotion, which is a rarity in a lifetime that will be filled with obligations or commitments born from external forces. The act of marriage is staking a claim for the life you want in the face of cynics and skeptics. It's choosing love, light, emotional security, and faith in each other above all else. That's powerful stuff! A marriage is bigger than the sum of its parts. It's not just two people joining their lives. It's two people illuminating each other to be the most vibrant, potent version of themselves, which is a gift in and of itself. The illuminated you and the illuminated them creates new potential for you as a couple, but also as an individual. Who you can be and what you can do with your time here on Earth grows exponentially when you are supported by the person who inspires you most. The life you can build together in a marriage where you each take your personal dreams and work together to help achieve them is a bond like no other. The mutual goals you set in your life and work toward, the shared victories and defeats you experience, and the path you carve together is a legacy immeasurable by any other scale. Marriage is epic and should be treated as such.

In writing this book, our intention is to communicate the hidden importance of the often-overlooked little things that are the foundation of conflict yet to come. We, ourselves, breezed over these pebbles not foreseeing the boulders that they would snowball to become over time. The historical resentments and patterns that can demolish a marriage usually start out as something seemingly unimportant. An assumption here. An accommodation there. An omission, an unclear boundary, a selfish act, an inconsideration, etc. These little things, these seemingly tiny tremors, have a rolling aftershock that can gain significant magnitude over time. Our hope is that you can glean some insight from our words and own experiences that will make you more mindful as you travel the marital path. Harmony is the result of diligent awareness, not just luck or chemistry, and not as easy to maintain in longevity as it is at the beginning.

Regardless of the current divorce rate statistics, when you are struck by the undeniable certainty that you want to marry someone, a profound visceral wave engulfs you and consumes you like nothing comparable. Once that happens, getting on the road to marriage almost becomes an obsession. You can't quiet a heart that is desperate with the kind of love that marriage inspires. Anyone who has felt it knows it's true.

• • • •

TO ENGAGE OR NOT TO ENGAGE

People get engaged presumably because they want to get married. But let's take a closer look at what the motivating factors are that urge people toward getting engaged. If we were playing a game show version of this where we had to buzz in and answer this question, the answers would vary wildly by contestant.

GAME SHOW HOST: One hundred people surveyed, name the top three reasons people get engaged.

CONTESTANT #1: To lock that shit down!

CONTESTANT #2: One of them said that the relationship had to move to the next level—so either get engaged or break up.

CONTESTANT #3: Her biological clock is ticking, and they need to get the baby-making party started if they want to have a family together because the fertility struggle is real.

CONTESTANT #4: Because they can't imagine living their lives without each other!

Contestant number four's answer is the one that we all hope for and has the best shot at actually having a marriage that goes the distance, but they are all valid and frequent motivations for getting engaged. No judgment. All answers are valid and welcome.

An engagement is truly the testing ground of marriage compatibility. It's the last exit before being legally bound. Being engaged is a significant level up from boyfriend-girlfriend, boyfriend-boyfriend, girlfriend-girlfriend—you get the picture. It's a promotion in position and title to Fiancée (or Fiancé) that sends the message to all that you're really doing this. You start to play house, make more definitive couple plans, and are, in most cases, headed for an actual date where you will be married. Subconsciously, it's like putting your toe in the marriage pool to see if you really want to go in. Stand at the edge of the pool too long and chances are you won't go in or you have to pull someone in with you. Jump in too soon and you may not be prepared for how cold the water is. That doesn't mean that those marriages will fail, but there should be a natural, gradual, mutually agreed upon pace that you guys set before that final step. Mutual agreement is the most important part; keeping your marriage from sucking starts and ends with mutual agreement. When you trace back almost any major problem in a marriage it starts with one party feeling like the other didn't consider them above or along with themselves.

• • • •

INTENTION

Marriage is the beginning of a lifelong daily practice of presence, love, service, trust, adaptation, curiosity, self-care, and forgiveness undertaken only by those who see fit to do so. It is not a mandate, it need not be a norm, and it is the most highly personal thing that you will ever do with another person, and no one, absolutely no one, can decide what's right for you both. Your marriage is not a public trust. It is a private and sacred bond between you two. The goal is to make your marriage thrive, not just survive. Intention is everything. You must set your intention for your marriage and then work toward it every day. A happy marriage isn't something you find; it's something you make. Marriage isn't a 50-50 enterprise; it's 100-100. It takes everything you've got. Giving half won't cut it. Don't be afraid to be the one who loves the most or works the hardest at keeping your marriage from sucking.

i know i want to make you mine

WE ALL HAVE THE same range of emotions, and while our experiences are unique to us there is something universal to the process and evolution of a marriage, beginning with the decision to get engaged. There are legendary proposals, great proposals, good proposals, mediocre proposals, and downright disappointing proposals. All proposals proclaim, "I know I want to make you mine!" and change the trajectory of your life forever. It's ripping off the floaties and diving into the deep end with the one you love. May the Love Gods always be on your side as you start not just a new chapter but rather a new book called *The Two of Us Against the World*.

• • • •

THE PROPOSAL

It all starts with the proposal. The proposal sets the tone for everything to come in the marriage that you want to *not* suck in the long run, so it benefits the both of you lovebirds to try to make it special.

Finding the love of your life is monumental. You know it because it feels monumentally different than every other relationship you've been in. It feels so good, in fact, that it can often make you feel sick with "I must lock this thing down immediately" panic. Getting engaged is truly awesome when you get engaged to the right person. How do you know it's the right person? Well, the "right person" is the exact opposite of the wrong person, which is every other person you've dated up until this point in your life. That's not to say you dated losers, you just didn't date this person who does all the right and surprising things that bring out the person you didn't know, but always imagined, you could be. You feel invincible. Life is amazing. There is beauty all around you. You are filled with a joy you never knew before. It is unlike any other experience you will ever have. And if you happen to get engaged more than once to someone you love deeply, then you'll have these feelings more than once. And good for you. Enjoy it every time.

GET YOUR TRAILER MOMENT:
a cautionary tale
by amiira

THERE ARE SEMINAL moments in your life, moments that you will retell to your friends, parents, children, and grandchildren, that make up the "Story of You." These are the "Trailer Moments" of your life. If your lives were cut together to make a movie trailer, the big marquee moments would be what made the cut. The moment someone asks you to marry them most certainly makes it into the Movie Trailer of your life. Whether you saw a marriage proposal romanticized in movies or television or some big celebrity was splashed across the cover of a tabloid with a giant rock on her finger, you have been groomed/programmed to know that getting engaged is a BIG DEAL. It's a Trailer Moment. And there is a "RIGHT" way to get engaged. Just ask anyone who got engaged the wrong way—they will tell you. Having a sucky proposal story is a monumental let down that may never be forgotten. NEVER. Know why? It's a big fucking deal because people who got engaged "the right way" talk about it a LOT, which only amplifies that you got cheated out of your big, special Movie Trailer moment.

Don't try to downplay the importance of the proposal. It's a big deal. Not because I say so or because society says so, but because by not giving your special person some version of the right kind of big deal for them specifically, you have lessened their Life Story. Every time she thinks of her proposal, she won't feel overwhelming twinges of joy; she'll feel sad and disappointed. Or even worse: When someone asks her how she got engaged, she'll feel embarrassed to tell the story of how lame it was, and then, on top of that, she will have to make excuses for you to her friends, family, and sometimes strangers to protect you from people who will judge you for being lame. Do you know how shitty it feels to have to make excuses to strangers? I'm telling you from experience. I've been engaged twice and neither of my husbands had their shit together at proposal time. I have yet to have a good proposal, and it's quite possibly cause enough for me to dump husband number two and roll the dice so that I might get a Trailer Moment proposal before I bite the dust. I've been cheated out of a great moment in life, and I know it!

My first proposal came in Las Vegas after a Social Distortion concert when my boyfriend blurted out, "We should get married. If I'm ever going to marry anyone, it's going to be you, so why not do it now?" We then set out to find wedding bands, procure a marriage license, and make a reservation at the Graceland Wedding Chapel. An Elvis impersonator did the deed of joining us in our young and impulsive matrimony. It took us three or four days to get everything together because we didn't know about the marriage license, and that courthouses are closed some hours. This in and of itself gets to be a Trailer Moment in my life because we ran around Las Vegas like young and in love crazy people in a romantic comedy. The beginning of the end where everyone except the two people in the movie can see that these two aren't going to make it if they can't figure this part out.

My second proposal Greg and I discuss in detail later.

You're reading this book because you want to have a happily ever after kind of life with the person that you love most, and that starts with at least a good proposal, if not a great one, for your Trailer Moment. Sometimes you must do your part to get the life you want. So be the person that communicates your proposal desires to the person you hope is going to ask you "THE QUESTION." You'll be happy that you did in the long run.

Not all of us get "Meet Cutes" like in the movies. Sometimes your story is that you both were drunk and hooked up at a party then had sex before you knew each other's names. Or that you were on again/off again, waffling for years, looking for someone better, then ultimately realized that this is as good as it gets, so you settled in for the long haul. Neither of those are great in the retelling to Grandma Iris. You don't get to control the story of how you met or your early history of getting together, but you can have some control in this big moment in your lives. How you got engaged is within your control, so not seizing this opportunity is a total relationship foul if not a minor crime. A great engagement story that speaks to the depth of your relationship and love for each other will trump any unsightly hairy mole of a coming together that you may have had. Take the opportunity to paint a great picture of your love so you have something to tell your kids someday that makes you seem like the amazing people they think you are. Only the two of you really need to know the truth of how it all REALLY went down on that booze cruise in the Caribbean.

• • • •

PLANTING THE SEEDS

How do you let someone know that you want them to propose to you in a meaningful way without seeming like an arrogant and high-maintenance nightmare? Glad you asked. Here are a few suggestions to get you started in laying the groundwork for getting the Trailer Moment you deserve. Feel free to drop them into conversation with your mate when appropriate.

▶ Top moments in a woman's life are: driver's license, prom, losing virginity, getting her first dog, selling her first app, getting engaged, giving a TED Talk, getting married, selling her startup to Google, having a baby, winning the presidency, and randomly sitting next to a flirty A-List celebrity. If you're lucky you'll get to be a part of three of these moments, so best be prepared.

▶ I'm not expecting a super big deal when I get engaged, but I'm definitely expecting something more memorable than nothing. Ever heard the saying, "You get out of it what you put into it"? I want to have to find a way to give you back what you put into it. If you don't know what I mean, don't ask me to marry you.

▶ You should have seen Becca's ring. It's beautiful. Jonah took her to the place they had their first date and had the ring at the bottom of her champagne glass. Super unsanitary—please don't ever put surprises in my food— but that boy got serious brownie points for effort and straight up laid for the ring...repeatedly.

▶ I love you enough that I want you to succeed in everything that you do, so here's what I want you to know: When I get engaged, I want the moment to be special. It's the moment when you jump in with both feet, no safety net. I don't want to feel like I'm going to need a safety net. I want to feel like I'm with someone who knows how to get things done. Someone who swings for a home run when it matters. I don't want to marry the guy that's happy to lay down a bunt.

▶ If you ever want to know how to propose to me, here's a list of my favorite romantic comedies. Follow the breadcrumbs, Hansel.

• • • •

THE BEST PROPOSAL OF
ANYONE WE KNOW

We picked up our youngest daughter, Mighty, from school one day, and she was bursting to tell us about her exciting day. Here is the story, as told by Mighty Luna Behrendt.

Usually we get dismissed by grade to walk back to our classes, but fourth grade didn't get dismissed. We didn't know why we had to stay. Then we were told that we had to take a picture on the Lightning Field for the yearbook. When we all assembled for the picture, this guy came up to us and introduced himself as our teacher's boyfriend. Our teacher's parents were there, too, and the boyfriend was dressed up in a nice suit with striped socks. *(Note: Girls notice everything down to the socks. Our nine-year-old knew something was up because the boyfriend was wearing some "dress" socks.)* The boyfriend asked us if we would hold up these signs and stand in a row. When we all got our signs in position, my friend said, "Hey this says, 'Will You Marry Me?'"

The school principal, who had kept our teacher behind, walked her out onto the field. Then she saw the sign, her boyfriend, and her parents. She was so surprised that she turned pink and burst into happy tears. Her boyfriend walked over to her and got down on one knee, pulled out a ring box, and asked her to marry him right there. After she said yes, he put the ring on her finger. Then they hugged and kissed, and her parents came over and hugged them some more. We all ran to our teacher and huddled around her for one big giant hug, and the boys high fived her boyfriend for doing such a good job. It was awesome! I can't believe I got to hold the first "R" in Marry. I got to be part of something really special today, and I'm going to remember it forever.

Why this is the winner for us: This proposal pulled off what Gaylord Focker tried to do in *Meet the Parents*, which is one of our favorite movies. This proposal involved a tremendous amount of planning, scheming, and secrecy served up with the perfect amount of sentiment by including the teacher's parents and coworkers, as well as involving adorable children. This is what we consider a "Hero Proposal," and it's not normal. It's fantastic, but it's not what most people will ever get. We applaud the boyfriend for swinging for the fences and hitting the home run. That makes this marriage proposal our WINNER WINNER CHICKEN DINNER Proposal.

• • • •

THE BEST PROPOSAL: FIRST RUNNER-UP

Our friends, Brandi and Randall (Brandall, if you will), are that incredible, life-affirming combination of batshit crazy, completely original, and undeniably delightful. As individuals, they are big personalities, and together they are one cape shy of being crime-fighting superheroes, or magicians. Brandi and Randall had been dating for a few months and weren't living together yet, just having an occasional sleepover—just to give you an idea of the relative newness of the relationship.

One morning, Brandi woke up after having the weirdest dream. She told Randall, "I had the craziest dream. We were at my dad's house visiting for Father's Day, and I was asleep in my childhood bedroom. You woke me up, and you were dressed up like the unicorn stuffed animal I had on my bed when I was little.

It was white with pastel rainbow-colored hair, but it was you inside the unicorn costume. There were three birthday cakes in my favorite colors—a lavender cake, a pink cake, and a baby blue cake—and two big helium balloons. But it wasn't my birthday, it was Father's Day. My dad was holding the lavender cake, my mom was holding the pink cake, and you were holding the baby blue cake. You told me to have a bite, but there were no knives to cut the cake or plates or forks. So, I jammed my hand right in the middle of the lavender cake and pulled out a fistful of cake and a note that said, 'Will.' Then I jammed my hand in the middle of the pink cake and pulled out a fistful of cake and a note that said, 'You.' Then I jammed my hand into the middle of the baby blue cake and pulled out a fistful of cake and a note that said, 'Marry.' Then I took the pin out of the dried corsage from my high school prom that's still on my vanity mirror, and I popped the first balloon. A note dropped out that said, 'Me?' Then I popped the second balloon, and a ring fell out of it."

Brandi and Randall had a laugh over the weird dream. Then they went about their lives for the next two and a half years. One year, Brandi and Randall went to visit Brandi's parents for Christmas (not Father's Day, FYI), and on their third night there, Brandi was awakened by Randall dressed in a unicorn costume standing in her childhood bedroom with her parents, three cakes, and two helium balloons. When Brandi awakened, she was super confused in a déjà vu way...until things clicked in her brain.

That clever and romantic gem of a human being pulled off the crazy dream marriage proposal that will go down in their own personal infamy. Brandi was dumbfounded and giddy with disbelief when she gleefully jammed her hand into each cake searching for her notes and no one minded the mess she made. After she popped her balloons, got her ring, and kissed her new fiancé, they all ate cake in the middle of the night. It was awesome and weird. Just like Brandi and Randall.

Why this is the first runner-up: While there was some definite planning to pull off this fantastical proposal, it only really involved getting Brandi's parents in on the surprise. The cakes were made by Brandi's mom, and the costume and balloons were acquired from a local party and balloon store. While it was a big proposal, it was also a very private one that was literally the proposal of her dreams.

• • • •

THE BEST PROPOSAL: HONORABLE MENTION

Tyler and Mikki came from completely different backgrounds. Mikki grew up in the posh Palisades of Los Angeles and Tyler in a rundown industrial town in the Midwest. Tyler had avoided taking Mikki to his hometown, afraid that she'd change her mind about him if she saw where he came from. Finally, Mikki gave Tyler an ultimatum: Take me home to meet your family or we're done. Tyler and Mikki went to Tyler's hometown to visit his parents and brothers for Thanksgiving. Tyler forewarned Mikki that they were a loud, unruly bunch that drank and cursed too much. He told her about growing up, getting in trouble, getting arrested, feuding with the school jocks, working at the donut shop, and "The Bridge." The Bridge was where Tyler and his brothers would vandalize the high school spirit banners. The cheerleaders used to hang a banner on the underpass of The Bridge on game day that read, "GO DEVILS." Tyler and his brothers would spray paint an added sentiment, so it would read, "GO DEVILS, EAT ASS!" It was childish and dumb, but they did it every time. It was tradition.

Tyler was incredibly nervous during the visit, thinking that Mikki might fall out of love with him because of his family. The day before they were to fly home, Tyler's mom suggested he take Mikki around town to show her all his old haunts. Tyler and Mikki drove around town to his high school, the donut shop, the bar he and his brothers used to sneak into, and the river. On their way home, Mikki asked to see The Bridge again.

As they approached The Bridge, Tyler could see that someone had hung a sign. As they got closer the words came into focus. In big, bold letters was the message, "Tyler, Will You Marry Me?" However, the words "Marry Me" had been crossed out and re-placed with the spray-painted words, "Eat Ass!" Tyler nearly drove off the side of the street when he spotted his entire family standing on The Bridge laughing. They had all been in on it. Mikki had contacted Tyler's family earlier and hatched a plan. It ended up being the perfect proposal for the whole family.

Why this is the honorable mention: This seems like it's right out of a John Hughes movie and is super sweet, but it only gets Honorable Mention because Tyler should have manned up and had a little more faith in his girlfriend, even if he didn't have any in his family. Bonus points go to Mikki for being bold enough to do the proposing and finding a way to squash all the bad reputa-tions that Tyler was holding about his family and his hometown in one fell swoop. While it may look like this was a big proposal, in reality it was family holding a sheet over the side of an over-pass. Sometimes very little is needed to have a big impact.

Note to the reader: These three marriage proposals won us over because of how well-suited the proposal was to the person it was meant for. A proposal doesn't have to be a public declaration or grandiose in any manner for it to be meaningful and effective.

THE TWO SIDES OF THE COIN

the upside of doing it right...

Regardless of any botched move you might make during your engagement and married life, you will always still be the guy that pulled off a great proposal. I can't tell you how much currency this carries. When you've fucked up majorly and she's questioning why she ever even married you, there will be a small part of her that flashes back to her engagement, her magical special moment when you proposed, and it will fill her deflated balloon back up a little bit—maybe even enough for her not to dump your sorry ass.

the downside of doing it right...

If you're a guy who can pull off an awesome and romantic proposal, which takes an actual plan with elements of execution, then why can't you pick your underwear up off the floor ever?

the upside of doing it wrong...

You've set the bar so low that she doesn't even expect you to be able to pick your underwear up off the floor. Seriously, dude, your only job is to keep breathing.

the downside of doing it wrong...

You're the guy who didn't even have it together to plan a decent proposal. You clearly may be someone who can't be trusted with any major responsibility. Homie don't wear the pants in this house. *P.S. We know "Homie" is a word used by old people—we were there when they invented it.*

the bad proposal

WHEN YOU COME OUT of the gate with a bad proposal, you're planting one of the biggest marriage landmines that will explode in your face again and again. It's starting your marriage in the hole so that when you hit suckage in the future, your person has that landmine to step on.

"I should have known when the proposal sucked that the marriage was going to."

"What did I expect from the person who couldn't even manage a decent marriage proposal?"

Here's the problem with a bad proposal: Unless you are drunk or on drugs, you're insanely conscious of it happening all wrong. So even while your mouth is saying, "Yes," or, "Oh, my God!" your brain is saying, "NO!" or, "Oh, shit!" or, "Please don't ask me to marry you like this!" or, "Why are you wrecking everything?" or, mostly, "Please shut up, please shut up, please shut up!" You are so acutely aware that this is a bad proposal that it fills you with all the wrong feelings. Instead of excitement, you feel anxiety. Your "flight" reflex is activated because you're now in the middle of an internal crisis in which you firmly have a shadow of a doubt or even a full doubt that this person can't take care of you or handle the big shit. That's the truth.

In the absence of a grand romantic gesture to pump endorphins through your body and make you take leave of your brain and all logical thought, what you have left is fear—and lots of it. Fear of commitment, fear of the future, fear of making a mistake, fear of getting trapped, fear that you don't even really like this person, fear that you're settling for a buffoon. When someone asks you to marry them, you immediately feel obligated to say yes, even if you want to say no. Who wants to be the one to crush a vulnerable human being offering you their heart when they clearly think that you're on the same forever soul mate page as they are? It sucks to say no to a marriage proposal, so we as human beings generally don't. Do you know how many engagements are broken? In a recent study the actual number was a shit ton of them. Know why? Because the yes was not a genuine "I can't imagine living my life without you" yes. It was an obligated "Oh crap I don't want to break his heart today or break up with him, so I'll say yes now and get out of this later if I need to" yes.

Bad proposals take place in their own weird, surreal time that is simultaneously so slow that your mind races a million miles an hour with every dreaded thought possible and so lightning fast that you feel like you've already waited way too long to answer and must answer quickly. Your brain is both a mushy mess and firing every neuron.

We know this emotional and mental maelstrom first hand. The problem with being proposed to badly is that, if you decline said bad proposal or ask your loved one to try again another time after they've put some thought and effort into it, you risk wounding their ego and their feelings to such a degree that it might turn into the beginning of the end. If your marriage proposal sucks, you're already starting out in the hole.

We want you to get to have a good engagement, so you may need to take some of the responsibility in making that happen, whether that's enlisting a friend to clue in your mate on the need for a promising proposal or having a straightforward conversation with your person about what you want—it's up to you to plant the seeds if you suspect it's the only way you're going to get flowers.

• • • •

OUR ENGAGEMENT: GREG'S SIDE OF THE STORY

The story of my proposal is so agonizing that it sits in my gut like a hibernating bear that awakens every time I'm asked, "So how did you and Amiira get engaged?" I start to open my mouth to recall the events of December 30, 1999, and the bear curls her lips, bares her sharp teeth, and digs her claws deep into my gut.

Amiira and I were in love. There was no question about that. We'd been dating for more than a year and officially together for more than nine months. We'd met and spent time with each other's parents. We'd discussed kids, careers, bands. We were, in my mind, right for each other. Well, she was right for me. I had never felt this kind of love for another person. Not the "I can't stop wanting to have sex with you kind," although that was part of it, but also the "I can see a future with you" kind. Amiira was just in a different league—still is.

She is the kind of woman who doesn't need a man to make her life whole, who can solve her own problems, and who is capable to a fault. It's the thing that makes her amazing to me. Sadly, it's also the thing that intimidates me and became the thing I most resented her for later in our marriage. *(Take note, young reader, that what we seek in our partner may be what we may be lacking ourselves.)*

There's been a lot written about knowing when you are ready to ask someone to marry you, from "when I have my ducks in a row," to "when I finish school" (which usually means maybe never), to "the heart wants what it wants...now." For me, I was overcome by this warm, all-encompassing feeling that this was my destiny. In my fantasies about Amiira, I was always able to see beyond the bedroom. When the idea of the girl of your dreams standing by an open minivan door holding a bundle of baby turns you on then you, my friend, are ready. To be clear, that doesn't mean you are ready to ask. That means you are ready to plan to ask. These are two different things, and that is where I made my mistake.

Let's go back over it. I was thirty-three and fairly well into a career as a full-time standup. I'd just had my first TV development deal for a sitcom and an HBO special. I wasn't leaving show business anytime soon. I was three years into my sobriety and had successfully lived on my own for more than a year, meaning I knew how to cook, clean, decorate, and pay bills...some of them on time. I owned my own car, and I had a valid driver's license. So, I had my shit pretty well together. I was by no stretch of the imagination wealthy, but I was viable, as they say.

If I'd had a proposal plan, I could have really done it right. Perhaps if I had waited another six months to propose I might have really pulled off something special that I'd look back on fondly. But I panicked and rushed it. Why? Partly because of the setting (we were staying in this crazy beach house on Diamond Head in Hawaii), and partly because I was so in love with Amiira.

But mostly because my mother was dying.

I know I just hit you with a major downer. Spoiler alert! My mother ended up living longer than expected, but at the time she had just been diagnosed with lung cancer, and we were unsure of how long she had to live. And I was in a bit of a hurry for her to see me happy.

My mother was an odd duck. She was tough and smart and hard to figure out. She never liked anyone I dated, ever. Ever! She didn't hate them. She was always kind, but then she'd say in private, "That's not going to happen. Just get a job." She was a pragmatist, to say the least, and not much of a romantic. She had never expressed a desire to see either my sister or myself married, let alone have kids, until our lives seemed at least somewhat sorted out. My mother loved that I was a performer, and she knew a performer's life was hard and took commitment, and she didn't want anything getting in the way of that.

But, boy, did her eyes light up when Amiira was around.

My mother got positively giddy. It was weird. She got uncharacteristically excited. Her excitement was another indicator to me that Amiira was the one. My dad liked her too. He pretty much likes everyone, but even he could be heard bragging about Amiira to the boys at his club. But ever since we found out about Mom, it had been dark at home, and, of course, I thought this would also help to bring some light.

Back to the proposal...

I made the decision to propose just days before leaving for Hawaii. One evening shortly after Christmas, sitting by the fire with my mom and dad, I broached the subject knowing they'd both be psyched. My mother had told me years before that she had been given her mother's wedding ring. I had assumed she told me that little nugget of information as shorthand for "the ring is mine when the time comes," and she'd pass it on to me to give to Amiira. Otherwise, why tell me about it in the first place?

But my mom was an odd duck and rarely predictable. So, I told them my intentions, and they were indeed happy. My mom even got teary, and my dad looked at me almost as if to say, "Thank you." Both Mom and Dad were psyched about my decision. I told them I hadn't had time to get a ring, so my mother excused herself to get something from the other room. I assumed she went to fetch the RING—her mother's wedding ring. But instead, she returned holding an ornament from our Christmas tree. It was a male angel with a comically big nose holding out a pink heart all made of clay. I was totally confused.

"You can give her this," Mom said, seriously.

I tried to hide whatever ten thousand things were happening to my face. Mom said something like, "It's not being about a ring, and it's about the moment and the ring is a token, and if she loves me she'll know I can't afford a ring right now..." blah blah blah... the gesture of love, something about crafts.

My mother was a great lover of crafts, but this hardly seemed like a suitable replacement for a diamond engagement ring.

"Um, okay," I said, not knowing if my bride was an "I like a ring" or "I don't need a ring" kind of girl. I didn't know. I'd never asked. I hadn't done the research. I didn't even know there were different cuts of diamonds. Amiira had been married before— maybe she was totally over diamond rings and it was passé.

But I'm a romantic. I should have just said, "Mom, this is not how I ever imagined getting engaged. This almost feels like I'm challenging her to accept less."

But that's not what I said. She was my mom. She was sick. I was more worried about her than my bride to be. So, I said, "Cool."

And so, I was off to Hawaii to join Amiira's entire family with an engagement ornament...you know, like in the movies.

The conversation I had with Amiira's parents went well. And I was proud of myself for even consulting them in the "anti-everything" era of the late '90s where everyone I had surrounded myself with was too cool to be seen doing anything even slightly traditional. Sitting down with Bill and Sharon was an aberration. But I was clear and firm with them; I'd come to love Amiira, and I was excited about my prospects as an entertainer. I felt I could take care of her and knew I could love her forever. I used those words.

Here's the thing: I wasn't ready, but I had made up my mind. I've seen people do this at standup open mic nights. They are convinced they can go onstage and just talk and be funny without preparing, that their "people think I'm funny at work" personality will carry the day. It doesn't. It's always a heartbreaking disaster. Even the most natural-looking performer in the world prepares. I guess I thought charm—or my smile, or my stammering lack of a point, or lack of an actual question (like, say, "Will you marry me?")—would carry the day.

I'm not going to give the play-by-play here, but the short of it is: I didn't plan anything. I hadn't written down or practiced a proposal. I just said a bunch of words. She said, "Are you asking me to marry you?" I said yes.

Then I gave her a clay ornament. I'm not even sure she said yes.

Ugh.

My proposal wasn't just a squandered opportunity. I robbed the person I love most in the world of a great moment—a great moment for both of us. We were in one of the most idyllic spots in the world, and instead, I proposed in this weird beach house rental bedroom. I didn't have choice words, and I didn't have the ring that I knew deep in my heart she wanted. I didn't have anything except what I wanted, which was to see my mother happy before she died. Even this, I'm sorry to say, is no reason to botch your proposal.

I think even my mother would agree.

In the end, she said yes, and there were some conditions and conversations to be had, which we address later in the book. Later, I did a "do over" and proposed with my grandmother's ring and lit candles in Amiira's house. But, alas, the bad proposal isn't a thing I'll ever get to take back.

● ● ● ●

OUR ENGAGEMENT: AMIIRA'S SIDE OF THE STORY

I did not plant the seeds for a good engagement (see page 19), and, as a result, there were no flowers. Why didn't I plant the seeds? I wasn't expecting things to move so fast and was still feeling out the relationship for forever potential. To be honest, I wasn't totally sure that Greg was marriage material *for me*. I had been married once before, so I was feeling extra cautious about who I was going to legally shackle myself to again.

Certainly, I could have said no—possibly should have said no—or at least I certainly should have put the brakes on and been clear about what I wanted and needed, but that's not how I handled Greg's proposal because I really wasn't sure what to do.

Half of my family lives in Hawaii, which is not a terrible place to be obligated to visit relatives. As the dawn of the new millennium approached, my family had decided that we all wanted to be together on New Year's Eve. No one in my family has a big enough house to accommodate all of us, so my parents rented a large house near Diamond Head. Greg and I, being in our first year together, were excited to spend New Year's together.

The weather was mostly beautiful, with the occasional brief tropical shower and the occasional dumping of monsoon weather. The air smelled like tuberose and plumeria, the skies were the bluest blue, and from the balcony off the living room you could see schools of dolphins frolicking in the ocean. Greg and I had a bedroom with floor to ceiling windows, sliding doors that overlooked the ocean, and had a private balcony. There was also access to the pool area and the general outdoors where you could overlook the ocean or even walk down the rocks to it. The bedroom, much like the rest of the house, had uninspiring and outdated décor.

It's important to give these descriptions because I want you to understand that there were opportunities for the proposal to be romantic. We had access to an ocean and the moonlight or even just an ocean view; plus, we both had working legs to get us to the outdoors. But that's not what happened.

We did not get engaged on the beach in Hawaii, or under the glorious moon in Hawaii, or even outdoors in Hawaii, even though we were in Hawaii, one of God's most glorious accomplishments. We got engaged in a bedroom that had stuccoed walls, with wall-to-wall carpet that always felt damp and slippery under our feet, while I was in a bed with an ugly patterned bedspread.

Greg and my parents were upstairs hanging out, and I had already gone downstairs to read a compelling book that I was dying to finish. Greg and my parents enjoy each other's company immensely, so I thought nothing of it when he stayed upstairs with them. I was in bed reading quite contently for a while when Greg came into the room. He wanted to know what I was doing. I was so engrossed in my book that I didn't even really look up when he came in. I think I muttered a sarcastic response because what I was doing was obvious, and I was in the zone.

Greg kept talking to me—stammering really—and not making any sense. I was clearly reading and didn't want to be disturbed. But Greg was not picking up on the signs and continued to distract me, much to my chagrin. I finally put down my book, not bothering to mask my annoyance. I did not understand what was happening, or what he wanted from me, and so I tried hard to key in.

I struggled at first because Greg was rambling and asking rhetorical questions:

"We're best friends, right?"

"We like to hang out."

Were he not a sober man, I would have thought he was high on something. I began to realize that he was attempting to propose to me.

"I think we should always hang out forever. Like, when we're old."

Not only was it not going well, but I was not psyched about it. I felt the panic rise in my chest making it nearly impossible to breathe. My only thoughts were, "Shit. Shit. Shit. This is happening. No, don't be doing it like this."

Greg was clearly panicking, and I knew instantly that he was asking me to marry him because of his mom. He had just come from being with her, and he was scared. This was about his mom, not me.

Greg's mom had been diagnosed with Stage 4 lung cancer and was about to have half of one lung removed and then dive into an intense course of chemotherapy. Her prognosis was that she'd be lucky to live five years. Instantly I knew that Greg wanted to lock down some happiness and peace of mind for his mom. It has to be hard for a mother to know that she's dying and that neither of her adult kids are married.

I was a woman with a job, some savings, and a stable and decent family. Hitching his wagon to mine would take a load off for his mom and give her the distraction of a wedding. All of these thoughts raced through my mind in five seconds. Finally, I asked the obvious question.

"Are you trying to ask me to marry you?"

Relieved, he nodded, eyes wide in fear. I felt bad for him. I felt bad for his mom. I felt bad for me. I took a deep breath, trying to calculate my next move. I don't have to do anything until he brings out the ring, I told myself. So, I waited and tried to decide what to do. I did love him, and I knew that it was a definite possibility that I could end up wanting to marry him. The problem was it was too soon to tell. Six months from now we could be engaged or broken up—who knows?

But we didn't have six months to see where the natural course of our relationship would take us. This was happening now. I waited for him to ask me to marry him and bring out a ring. He waited expectantly. It was a standoff. What was happening? Did he think he had asked me already? Is he waiting for my answer? He hadn't asked me anything!

Greg finally realized that he hadn't actually asked me to marry him. Then he handed me a Christmas ornament. It was a cartoonish bald guy with a giant nose in a white robe holding a pink heart between his cartoon clay hands. I took the "angel" ornament from him and looked at it quizzically.

"See, he's giving you his heart," Greg said.

I told him that I thought it was cute and waited nervously for him to pull out the ring and propose. Eventually it became clear to me that there would not be any ring giving going on. Huh? I genuinely didn't know what to do or what to say, and I definitely didn't know what the hell had just happened.

"It doesn't seem like I'm engaged. Until I am asked the question and there's a ring on my finger, as far as I'm concerned, I'm not engaged," I thought.

Satisfied with that, I went to bed and pretended to read while internally I freaked out and didn't sleep a wink that night.

The next morning my parents looked at me expectantly as we prepared breakfast. Well, they asked? Well what? They were genuinely surprised that I hadn't come running into their bedroom last night and jumped on their bed to tell them the good news. I admitted that I wasn't sure if there was good news because I was rather confused as to what transpired the night before. There wasn't a marriage proposal, and there was no ring on my finger.

The more I replayed the bad proposal in my mind the less I wanted to marry Greg. The bad proposal just amplified any doubts I had and left me with the feeling that I had an "out." I didn't have to marry Greg because *technically* I wasn't engaged. When we were out shopping one day shortly after our "engagement," Greg bought me a silver Hawaiian bangle bracelet that read "Ku'u'ipo," which means sweetheart in Hawaiian. This will be instead of a ring he told me—an engagement bracelet. Engagement bracelet? And one that cost $40 from a street vendor in Waikiki? I don't think so. I tried to roll with the engagement bracelet, but I wasn't feeling it. It didn't feel special. It didn't feel meaningful.

Finally, I confessed to Greg that I was embarrassed to tell anyone that I was engaged because the first thing anyone wants to see is THE RING. That's it. They want to ogle it with envy or judge the shit out of it in snarky bad form. Until there was a ring on my finger, I didn't feel engaged. Quite honestly, I deserved an engagement ring, and not necessarily a huge honking diamond. I wanted to be properly proposed to; otherwise, the engagement didn't feel real. The symbolism and the token of an engagement ring is meaningful to every woman I know. The reason most jewelry stores stay in business is due to the sale of engagement rings. When you think about a wedding you think Dress, Vows, Rings, Kiss, Cake. That's the deal. Those are the necessary components. When we time travel to the future when the new equation is Jumpsuit, Nod, Text, Handshake, and Pudding then maybe I'll feel differently, but I'm still in this era where every woman in my personal historical marital lineage has a ring on her finger.

A couple months later Greg went for a do-over. He lit a bunch of candles in my house, had his grandmother's ring, and formally asked me to marry him. In the months that had passed I had given the idea more thought and knew for sure that I did want to marry him. But believe me, if he hadn't at least attempted to redeem himself with a do-over everything most likely would have ended differently. I know myself well enough to know that I would have continued to have been haunted by the bad proposal and been filled with doubts over him as a man that I could depend on to handle the big stuff in life. It's the truth. That's how my mind works; it doesn't mean that other women are like me. But if you've watched television, movies, advertisements, or read any literature at all, then you have a vague (if not crystal fucking clear) idea of what a proposal is meant to look like. I wondered, if Greg couldn't pull off a decent proposal, how could he save our family from a house fire?

Remember, I had failed at marriage once before, so I was being uber cautious and super gun shy about walking down the aisle again. Lucky for me, Greg wanted to make our engagement memorable for us in a better way. Otherwise, I might have sabotaged getting to have an incredible partner for life and having the best kids in the world.

• • • •

THE WORST PROPOSAL OF ANYONE WE KNOW

Besides my own proposal story, my friend Willow's is the worst. Willow is an artistic soul who makes things with her hands—paintings, photography, knitting, jewelry, terrariums, music, poetry...you get the picture. She's super bohemian, swims against the stream of corporate America, and couldn't pass up a unique find if her life depended on it. Willow's the person who goes on silent retreats, takes ecstatic dancing classes, and studies with a shaman. You can even imagine her as someone who dresses like a magical character out of a children's book series because she does.

One day, Willow and Ben, her boyfriend of a couple of years, were both leaving the house to go their separate ways—her to yoga, him to the recording studio. Shortly after leaving the house, Ben pulled his car alongside her car as they were driving down a busy main thoroughfare in Los Angeles. He rolled down his car window and started yelling something at Willow as he drove what felt dangerously close to her own car. Willow rolled down her window and strained to hear what he was yelling as they continued driving on the busy street.

Ben yelled, *"Let's get married!"*

Willow yelled back, *"What?"* She was sure this wasn't happening.

Ben yelled back, *"Will you marry me?"*

Willow was stunned by the question and took her foot off the gas for a moment as she processed what he said. Suddenly, she was rear-ended by an Escalade whose driver jumped out of the car and began yelling expletives at her for slowing down. The boyfriend, not noticing the accident, drove away, pleased with his spontaneous action. After Willow and the Escalade driver exchanged insurance information, she called her boyfriend to let him know what happened. The boyfriend barely registered what she said because he was excitedly begging her to come meet him at the mall.

Willow, not knowing how or what to feel, drove her smashed-up car with the bumper dragging to the mall. Her boyfriend met her by the escalators and led her to a chain jewelry store where he had picked out a platinum solitaire diamond ring that looked like every other ring in the store and that probably a million other women have. (Not to mention that Willow only wears yellow or rose gold jewelry and has a strong conviction against the atrocities of diamond mining.) He slipped the ring on her stunned finger, paid the clerk at the chain store, and then took her to get a Wetzel's Pretzel. Willow hadn't even officially said yes to his proposal.

When Willow retells her proposal story, she always ends with this: *"So I guess I'm engaged and now have a higher car insurance rate?"*

Willow and Ben hit some rough patches a few years into the marriage, and Willow stopped wearing the engagement ring because she never really liked it and there was nothing about it that felt like it was meant for her. As the marriage declined further, she used the proposal as proof that she shouldn't have married a man who clearly didn't care enough to really know her. Willow and Ben got divorced after two great years of marriage and five horrible ones. The proposal would have been cute in a movie about someone else, but it was entirely wrong for Willow, and it always shadowed over her like an ominous cloud.

• • • •

THE WORST PROPOSAL: FIRST RUNNER-UP

Jason thought that it would be cool to propose to Bethany while they were camping together for the first time. Bethany was outdoorsy and loved nature, so Jason figured that, if they were in nature, the right moment would present itself, and he'd wing it when the muse struck. The first day of their camping trip it became clear that Bethany was the more experienced camper, so Jason followed her lead easily. She knew how to set up camp, how to fish, how to cook over a campfire, and how to survive in the outdoors.

On their third night, under a full moon, Bethany fell asleep by their campfire. Jason took it as a sign and decided to spell out the words "Marry Me Bethany" in marshmallows, graham crackers, and chocolate bars that they had packed to make s'mores. He was delighted by the idea that she would awaken by the campfire and see the message written out in treats and then the ring box with the engagement ring he had picked out for her, with the velvet box opened so the diamond would shine by the firelight. To be clear: Jason spelled out "Marry Me Bethany" in FOOD on the ground OUTSIDE in the wilderness, where she slept, and left the ring box open. Jason then retired to the tent thinking she'd wake him up with her excitement upon finding the dream marriage proposal.

That's not what happened.

Turns out that critters like s'mores, too, and Bethany awoke to a family of raccoons eating the marshmallows, graham crackers, and chocolate. Bethany shouted for Jason, and, when he saw what was happening, he lurched for the ring box. One (or more) of the raccoons turned vicious and bit him on the hand.

Even though he broke a cardinal rule of camping (don't leave food open outside!), Bethany married Jason, and Jason got to experience a series of tetanus shots. They both lived happily ever so far.

Why this is first runner-up: Now it must be said that Jason did many things right. He really thought about what would be meaningful to Bethany, and then chose a time and location that suited who Bethany is perfectly. The originality of spelling out a proposal in s'mores ingredients was so adorable and charming, even though he did kind of endanger her life by decorating the area she was sleeping in with food. Usually the wilderness is where they keep the bears on this planet, so they got off lucky with only being accosted by raccoons.

• • • •

THE WORST PROPOSAL: HONORABLE MENTION

June and Elliot had been together for seven years. June had an apartment, and Elliot still lived with his parents but stayed at June's place most of the time. In January, June told Elliot that if he didn't propose by midnight on New Year's Eve, she was going to move on because she was ready to get married. If he didn't want to marry her, then she wanted to free herself up to find the person who did. In essence, Elliot had nearly a full year to get his act together or to cut bait.

HOW TO KEEP YOUR MARRIAGE FROM SUCKING

Every few months June reminded Elliot that New Year's Eve was the cut-off and, if he didn't have the intention to propose, to let her know so she didn't waste any more time. Elliot assured June that she wasn't wasting time. When New Year's Eve rolled around, June felt both nervous and excited. She knew he had a year to plan a proposal or a year to break up with her. On the day of the deadline, she anticipated something good. Nine p.m. rolled by, 10 p.m. rolled by, 11 p.m. rolled by.

June assumed Elliot would do something special at 11:59 p.m., and she became an anxious wreck. They weren't alone; all their friends were at the party, doing champagne toasts about the up-coming year. Some of the friends who knew of the proposal deadline sat expecting something great. Midnight passed without mention from Elliot, who was oblivious to anything, especially the waiting friends.

June took Elliot to a quiet corner and reminded him of the overdue proposal deadline. Elliot was genuinely taken aback—he had thought June was kidding about the proposal deadline. June burst into tears; she had been as honest and forthcoming as she could be, and, not only had Elliot not taken her seriously, he had strung her along all year.

June broke up with Elliot. In response, Elliot asked her to marry him. For a moment June thought the whole thing had been a ruse, and he was just making her sweat it out. But soon she realized that Elliot hadn't intended to propose. There was no ring, no speech, no effort, no thought. It was a knee-jerk marriage proposal to keep June from breaking up with him.

June gave Elliot a reprieve. He had one week to get a ring and propose properly or to get out of her life. (It should be said that Elliot's family had money, Elliot made money, Elliot could afford a ring comfortably with his bank account and credit history. And, in addition to specific directions from his girlfriend, he had two sisters that could offer the female perspective.) One week later, there was still no ring and no proper proposal.

Once again, June relented; she wanted to marry Elliot. She'd spent seven years with Elliot and imagined her future with Elliot. After many tears and Elliot begging for another chance, June gave him another week to pull it together. Elliot finally presented June with a ring. A family ring. June was overjoyed.

Now properly engaged, June started planning a wedding. But Elliot got cagey with wedding details; he wouldn't give June an idea of how many guests he'd invite to the wedding. June finally called Elliot's mother to ask for a ballpark figure on their side of the family for the wedding. Elliot's mother was shocked—this was the first she'd heard that Elliot and June were engaged; he hadn't mentioned it. When Elliot's mother learned that June was wearing a family ring, she demanded it back, declaring it stolen by her son and not his to give. June gave Elliot's mother back the ring and promptly broke up with Elliot.

June looks back at this part of her life as the "low self-esteem years." She now has two beautiful kids and is happily married to a kick-ass guy who knew he wanted to marry June after their second date—and knew how to propose. BTW, Elliot is still single. I know, hard to believe that no one has landed this gem.

Why this is an honorable mention: June is not the only woman we know to lay down the "propose or we're breaking up" gauntlet. Sometimes this ultimatum shines the light on the "fear of marriage" feelings and rids them like monsters hiding under a toddler's bed. However, more often it backfires and you end up coercing someone to marry you that didn't really want to marry you. Usually, when someone figures out that they didn't really want to marry you, they don't stay married to you. It's a high stakes gamble that might pay off in the short run but can wreck you in the long run. So be careful, high roller.

Note to the reader: Greg here! The examples earlier of The Best Proposal Blah Blah Blah...etc. and some of the ideas we proposed tend to be referred to as a public proposal. We chose them in part because we think they show great courage but also because they are easier and more fun to write about than a woman getting a ring in her poached egg with her breakfast in bed. But what I was attempting in my own life with Amiira was indeed a private moment proposal. I meant to surprise only her, not everyone at Coachella. We believe, in no uncertain terms, the proposal should fit the relationship you are in. It doesn't matter if it's breakfast in bed or a walk up a mountain trail, just as long as you don't rob yourselves of it being memorable. On our fourth Christmas, I gave Amiira an eternity band to sort of replace my grandmother's ring, which wasn't really her style and tended to get caught on everything. It was under the tree at her parents' house, with her parents there, and she burst into tears, which she is not at all prone to doing. It was a small and private moment and probably the one she had been hoping for. We don't think something has to explode—other than your heart—during the proposal.

Given our status as relationship authors who believe men should still be asking women out, you may think that only a man can pop the question. Not true. A couple that is meant to be together will be together no matter who gets on bended knee or does the asking. The proposal should fit the couple and be awesome no matter who takes the initiative. We're just warning you that this is a profoundly meaningful moment in the story of your marriage that is in your control. You will have a long line of experiences and obstacles that will be out of your control during the course of your marriage, so when you're given a guaranteed op-portunity to roll snake eyes or hit triple cherries, TAKE IT. A pro-posal of marriage is where you will either win or lose points in the eyes of your spouse...for all eternity.

PROPOSALS THAT ARE MOVIE CUTE, NOT REAL LIFE CUTE

- HAVING THUGS BLINDFOLD and kidnap your beloved from her workplace, throw her in the trunk of a car, and drive her to the park bench where you first kissed.
- ASKING HER TO marry you at her sister's engagement party, bridal luncheon, wedding, or reception. Don't wreck her loved one's big moment by stealing the spot-light. Don't be that guy. Find your own moment.
- ANYTHING THAT INVOLVES space and/or time travel or getting into an oversized cardboard box.
- RIDING A WHITE stallion through the lobby of the Plaza Hotel, having never been on horseback before.
- HAVING FRIENDS DON ski masks and fake mug your significant other, even if this "is a hold up because she's stolen your heart."
- HIDING THE RING in an unmentionable part of your body—unless you love going to the ER and meeting new people.
- TYING THE RING to your pet boa constrictor and mak-ing her feed Axl his lunch mice.
- ASKING THE QUESTION as she's getting married to someone else in a large church service because you loved *The Graduate*.

- ASKING WHILE IN the nude—she has to be able to tell her parents and your future children about this moment without them looking at you awkwardly.

PROPOSAL HOW-TO GUIDE

by greg

There are a few times in your life where you get to be a hero or a rock star, unless you happen to be a bonafide hero or rock star. And you would be a moron not to jump at the opportunity to be one for this particular day. The day you pop the question is no ordinary day. It's your very own made-to-order hero/rock star day. This is the day that will go down in infamy in your life story. Your heroics will spread through social media like wildfire and be whispered like folklore as you pass through a gaggle of women. If you take the time to plan a romantic way to ask the love of your life to marry you, you will be rewarded. Not only with the warmhearted, bursting-with-love feelings you will get from the natural opiates coursing through your veins when you see how truly happy you have made the woman you love—though that feels great—but also with other rewards from a great proposal. Once you've decided this is the love of your life and you've nailed down the ring (or the stand-in Starbucks gift card, or whatever else will make your love weep), it's time to master the two parts of the proposal.

● ● ● ●

PART ONE: THE ACT

The act doesn't have to be a grand extravaganza, though it can be. One night some friends and I had gone to see a movie at an indie film house in L.A. The lights went down and the trailers rolled. The second trailer was for a *Pulp Fiction* rip-off. It looked cool, it was shot well, but the ideas were pure Quentin. Suddenly, the star of the trailer—a bank robber in a mask—stopped, looked right at the camera, and, while taking off his mask, said, "Trista? In the third row? Will you marry me?" The house lights came up, the dude ran down the theater aisle with the ring, got on one knee, and asked again, "Will you marry me?" Trista was in total shock. The assembled audience applauded, and comedian and friend Kathy Griffin, who I was with at the time, burst into tears. It was truly a magical moment. I'm certain Kathy asked to see the "rock," because that's who Kathy is. Regardless of how the rest of her entire life went, the bride-to-be had an amazing story to tell.

Now this was obviously an epic feat. This guy had clearly done his homework. They, as a couple, must have a connection to film, and she would be open to a grand gesture. The dude nailed it. Do you need to shoot a major motion picture? Arrange a flash mob? A ballpark big screen? Not even. Special comes in all shapes and sizes, but here's the size it should absolutely come in: hers. What would blow her mind or take her by surprise? What's a memory you want her to have? Better yet, what's a memory of YOU that you want HER to have?

Let's try a little exercise: Imagine you are the studliest version of yourself—the movie version of you where you are at your most handsome, most sexually potent, most awesome. Pretend you're that guy. Now think of the love of your life, of the best her that deserves the very best from you. If you had unlimited funds and time to plan, what would be the dream proposal for you to orchestrate that not only speaks to who she is as a woman but also speaks to who you are as a man, as well as who the two of you are as a couple? Sky's the limit. Dream big because dreaming doesn't cost you a thing. But it gives you a jumping off point to start brainstorming. Remember, your love mostly just wants the proposal to come from the heart.

Christ, if I had just walked Amiira to the beach then I could have hidden a bottle of her favorite Pinot Grigio and had a Hawaiian dude in the sand playing Replacements songs on a ukulele because Paul Westerberg (lyrical genius of the Replacements) holds the key to her heart. Then I could have given her my grandma's ring that I had demanded from my mom (after I smashed that stupid clay angel ornament against the wall) as a placeholder for a ring to be named later. I would have given her a fake, hand-drawn road map of the life I had planned for us and said words ending with "AMIIRA, YOU ARE THE LOVE OF MY LIFE. Will you marry me?" At least she would have known what to say yes or no to.

• • • •

PART TWO: THE WORDS

That brings us to the second part. The actual words. Coming from someone who just told you he spat nothing at his soon-to-be-bride, why take it from me (and fair enough)? But as a professional public speaker and writer I can tell you that if I've learned anything over the years, it's this truth: The most immediate way to anyone's heart is through a serum called the truth. In twelve-step groups, most people, regardless of public speaking abilities, are asked to share. Here's the format: Tell us what it was like, what happened, and what it's like now. And I think that is a spectacular way to begin to formulate your ideas for a proposal. I filled in my answers below.

What was it like? Before I met you, Amiira, I was dating mostly girls that wore men's pants and didn't like the outdoors.

What happened? And then I met you and suddenly I discovered the sun. But also happiness and hope and endless possibilities because you seem to see those things. You bring things out in me I didn't know existed, and that, in turn, makes me want to do the same for you.

What's it like now? I can't see living life without you. Maybe you can see life without me, but I won't know until I ask you this. YOU ARE THE LOVE OF MY LIFE. Will you marry me?

And, brother, if you pull this off—even if you get shot down—you will still be legend. Fail big is what I've learned in my life. If she says yes (and this next part comes from my wife, honestly) there will be sexual rewards, some hardcore heavy-duty lovemaking. There's nothing like receiving a declaration of undying love and a beautiful ring to make a girl want to rock your world. Not that sexual rewards should be WHY you make a heroic effort to plan a memorable proposal, but I'm just saying that, while the proposal is really about the woman, the guy gets a little sumpthin' sumpthin' as well.

● ● ● ●

PART THREE:
THE RING

When it comes to the actual engagement ring, there can be a lot of pressure. While some choose to forgo the tradition of presenting an engagement ring, it's still the most popular symbol for an engagement in western cultures. The engagement ring is traditionally placed on the finger nearest the little finger on the left hand because at one time it was believed that this finger contained the *vena amoris*, a vein that led to the heart. Pretty nifty little fact, huh?

An engagement ring is the tangible representation of a formal agreement to a future wedding and is tremendously meaningful to both parties. The ring is the symbol of claiming one's mate and one's future, a source of pride and accomplishment. The ring is the symbol of unconditional love and promise for the future. Both acquiring and presenting the engagement ring mark a tremendous step in a person's life. It is the time when a person is living in the cusp of a new world with the power to change his or her stars in a tiny little box. Many stress greatly over the ring. It generally requires saving up for, unless you are such a baller that you have tons of Benjamins burning a hole in your pocket. It needs to be a ring that your person will love because they will wear it until death or divorce do you part. It doesn't have to be a gigantic honking knuckle-duster, but it does have to be beautiful and right for her.

A note to the naysayers: Even if you think your lady is not an engagement ring type, she probably is. Even if she says she doesn't care about a ring, she probably does. Even the least sentimental person you'll ever meet can be brought to tears by the unexpected beauty of the right ring for them. Chances are if your lady has downplayed the importance of a ring it's because she just wants you to fucking ask her to marry you already, and the ring presents an obstacle that she doesn't think you can get over. But, seriously, get a ring.

Ladies, if your person needs a hint, don't be afraid to dog-ear a page of a magazine. If finances are a consideration (as they are for most of us unlucky sods who aren't heirs to a family fortune) then you must get creative with your savings and be patient. How long to save and how much to spend on a ring is irrelevant—you have your own brain for that.

If you don't have a great sense of what kind of ring will really move your lady to her core, ask her closest confidants. They for sure will know and have opinions. They will teach you about Rose Gold and Peach Amethysts as an affordable and romantic alternative to traditional diamonds. You will get to see your lady's favorite celebrities' engagement rings. You will see more shapes, sizes, and settings of stones than you ever hoped to see. Your lady's confidants will accept this task with the utmost of seriousness and importance that it deserves. And you will get an education that will ultimately make you confident about pulling the trigger on the most symbolic piece of jewelry you will ever purchase in your life. Feeling the pressure? Good. You should want to get this right. You can always have a placeholder ring if you can't afford the ring you want to buy now. Know how you buy a starter home? Think of it as a starter ring.

• • • •

PART FOUR:
THE BLESSING

Since we're going through the exercise of doing this thing right, why not get the blessing from your lady or person's father, mother, sister, step-parent, Golden Retriever, or whomever is the former "guardian" of your beloved? Yes, it's old-fashioned and traditional, but so is an engagement, so why not just pony up and do it? Unless, of course, said former guardian is estranged or psychotic—then you can skip it. Seriously. Asking for the blessing is more than just a nice gesture toward the family; it lets them know that you take the caring for and well-being of their most treasured human as seriously as they do. Plus, you will get massive bonus points for including them from the beginning and giving them a nice story to tell their friends and relatives where you sound like a kick-ass stand-up person because, believe me, there will be times later when they talk shit about you. They can get cut out of the equation later, but let them have their moment as well early on and you will be endeared to them forever. Here, we'll give you a head start...Here are some good—and not so good—ways to go about getting a blessing.

GOOD

▶ "I love your daughter. I'm always going to love your daughter. I want to wake up next to her every day of my life, so I hope you'll be excited to hear that I'd like to ask her to marry me."

▶ "The only thing better than being a member of my family would be having the honor of being a member of yours and earning that right by taking care of your daughter every day for the rest of my life."

NOT GOOD

▶ "No one has ever done the things to me in bed that your daughter has. Her flexibility and willingness is off the charts. I'd like that to continue. With your permission, of course. I'm not a pig."

▶ "Would you rather get kicked in the stomach or the face? [Wait for answer.] Would you rather drown or burn to death? [Wait for answer.] Well I'm not going to do any of those things. Can I marry your daughter?...And then I thought we'd live at your house."

• • • •

PART FIVE:
WHAT IF YOUR PERSON SAYS "NO"?

It happens. We've seen it happen on jumbotrons, and we know it happens in private. What happens next is hard to say. If it's a straight out no, take a few weeks to drink and weep before you start to process the idea that you probably dodged a bullet. If someone says they have to think about it, you have to decide if this is how you want to start the rest of your life, in a relationship where you have more faith in them than they have in you. We don't have to really walk you through this because if the answer isn't yes, it's pretty much no.

Better to know that now than on your wedding day when they don't show up, or, even worse, after the birth of your second child when they want out. It's all painful and horrible, but it's better to know where you really stand before you have swum so far out that you can no longer see land. Know that you're going to be okay and probably even great someday. It won't be anytime soon but someday when you find your actual Favorite Person Ever you will be grateful that you got the "I Don't" instead of the "I Do."

And then it's up to the two of you to figure out how to proceed with the relationship, and you'll ask yourself a lot of questions. In our experience, most proposals and marriages were a foregone conclusion in both parties' minds before it even happened. That being said, we have gotten many letters from single people asking if they should "settle" and just marry someone they don't really want to marry just so they can be sure that they don't miss what might be their only opportunity to get married. That shit is real. Hearing no is not fun, but being with someone who thinks they are "settling" for you is a prison sentence.

• • • •

TO THE LADIES AND ALL POTENTIAL PROPOSEES

You are allowed to have expectations but remember that clinging too hard to them will set you up for a fall. Your person is not a mind reader. The idea that anyone should know your mind better than you or be able to sort things out the way you do is a notion that will not only make your engagement hard, it will follow you into your marriage and it will wreak havoc there, too. And trust me—in marriage, I need directions. I need to be guided sometimes, taught sometimes. I'm a quick learner, but I thrive under guidance. You don't have to tell him where to get a ring or that you'd like to get engaged looking at the Golden Gate Bridge from the headlands, but if you talk to him about jewelry or hint about San Francisco, well then maybe he's got a road map. We can't intuit you, but we can love everything about you. So, share it. More than once!

4

the engagement

ETTING ENGAGED IS MAGICAL and amazing. It's meant to be a great highlight in life and marks a time that is bursting with love, glory, invincibility, life, and hope. There will be plenty of terrible, stress-filled moments in your life, so it's important to really savor the great ones when you get them. Take a moment to remember how totally fucking incredible you felt when you were madly in love and newly engaged. Drink that shit in. It's a deep well you can revisit in tough times that will always make you remember the love you had for your person at the beginning. You should luxuriate in the experience of being engaged because planning a wedding is tough, no matter who you are, how much money you have, or how blessed an occasion it will be. Take your time with the engagement before planning your wedding.

Just be engaged for now. Just enjoy being engaged. Don't start planning your wedding today, this week, or even this month. Once you start, it is all you'll think about, so for now, just think about how great THIS is. Enjoy THIS. BE HERE NOW. Don't be in the future. Stop time travelling. Don't take on things you don't need to yet. Be in love. Be in light. Absorb this feeling on a cellular level because it is *magic dust* that helps you get through tough times in the future. Down the road, you can call on this feeling, this *magic dust*, of when things were bright, beautiful, and uncomplicated. When love was more prominent than fatigue and life was bursting with newness, not routine. This is one of the best parts of the movie of your life so luxuriate in it, feel the feelings of this time. Don't blow them away by dumping wedding planning feelings on top of them because those will crush these feelings, and then you won't get to have them. We spend so much of our lives rushing past our feelings and experiences to get to the next one. It's a terrible habit and this is the perfect time to break it. Put a pin in this feeling. Feel this feeling as much as you possibly can because this is one of those feelings that you won't want to forget and this feeling, the *magic dust*, will be the thing you recall when things get hard.

Because next comes planning a wedding, which can feel a bit like marriage boot camp. How you work together to handle all the different moving parts of a wedding will aid you both in dealing with the bigger things that will come later in your lives together. Planning a wedding and managing all the family members' feelings, egos, and needs, while still pushing your dreams to the forefront of the event, is a delicate and intricate dance. There will be times when you can't believe how great your life is, and there will times when you want to throw in the towel and elope. Ultimately, this gargantuan task will unite and bond the two of you in a way that is completely unique. It's as if you have to build an airplane that will fly out of things in your apartment. Some days it will feel impossible. Some days you will have minor setbacks and others, major victories. But when you finally get that bird up in the air, or rather, hear the first notes of "Here Comes the Bride" on your wedding day, you will feel invincible because the two of you got there together, and that's because you are an incredible team. It's the hardest you will ever work for a day you will barely remember.

rapid fire engagement
Q & A

Perhaps you've noticed by now that we're straight shooters (with a healthy dose of equal parts pure open heart and smart-ass), especially when it comes to matters of the heart. Engagement questions are among the most frequent ones we're asked, so here are our "first thing that comes to mind" answers to the questions that pop up most about engagement.

Q: How long should an engagement be?

A: A year. You need the year to plan. Everything over a year you lose the spark and excitement of the wedding. It becomes a looming monster, and you'll get on each other's nerves about it.

Q: How long is too long of an engagement?

A: A year and one hour. (Unless your fiancé is serving in the military, finishing their master's, out of the country building clean water wells for third-world nations, or otherwise actually unable to because of a real reason, not just laziness, "waiting for the right time," or procrastination.)

Q: How do you announce an engagement?

A: Bullhorn. We love an engagement party and love telling people in any way OTHER than on social media. Social media cheapens all things that are deeply personal. Think about how meaningful it is to get news from someone via their actual voice where you can hear and share in their excitement and emotions. Remember how good that feels? Do that.

Q: What have you announced by getting engaged?

A: That you don't want to die alone or have found the greatest person in the world for you, so hands off, grabby.

Q: What else have you announced by getting engaged?

A: That you're going into wedding planning overdrive and will speak of nothing else for the next year, so have patience with us because we know we are going to be unbearable.

• • • •

SORTING OUT THE HARD STUFF

Love is possibly the most powerful element on Earth. It is the fuel for all great things that human beings make—art, music, literature...other human beings. The fibers of love that bind you to another person are strong and seemly impenetrable in the beginning but can fade or be worn thin over time. You've seen the *Amazing Race*, right? There are always couples that start off being lovely, supportive, and complimentary about all the incredible qualities in their mate. Then, by the sixth country and challenge, the condescending tones come out, the voices are raised, and they are downright shitty to each other.

Dynamics change when pressure is applied and something important is at stake. In a marriage things that might not have seemed important at the beginning of your life together can take on new deeper meaning as time passes. Your relationship will certainly have to weather some storms. Some storms are minor and blow over quickly while others last for days or weeks and leave you with holes in your roof and no power. Then there are force-of-nature storms that can leave you near death not knowing where you could possibly go from here.

Things will bite you in the ass if you don't talk about them and sort them out before you get engaged. We once had friends who got married when they were in their twenties. The woman really wanted kids, and the man absolutely did not. They knew this about each other before getting married but got married anyway. It was the ultimate game of marriage chicken. Both sides were completely convinced that the other would come around and want the same thing they wanted. Ten years passed, the woman's biological clock started screaming, and the man had not changed his position on children in the least. He had been completely honest with her and she with him. Neither were at fault for lying, but both ended up losing because they got divorced over this massive difference in life plans.

The divorce wasn't an amicable one because both felt screwed over—he because he was never unclear about not wanting kids and she because she felt like she had wasted her fertile years on a dead-end marriage. Let this be something you think about with the gravity it deserves. If you and your partner are not on the same page on the big things, you need to figure them out before getting married. We're not saying don't get married. We're saying talk about it and come to a conclusion, compromise, or resolution that you both can live with without there being a giant resentment hanging over your lives.

Here is a quiz for you to take with your mate to get into the sticky bits that can be hard to talk about. Grab a couple sheets of paper and pens and write down your answers. Once you've answered each question, share your answers and see if you're completely in sync or if there's some talking to do. It's important that you are honest with yourself and each other on all the big things because if you start this union off withholding your truth, it will cause you nothing but trouble. What you're going for here is full transparency. Starting a dialogue is more important than being completely matched up on your answers. The conversations you will have on these topics will bring you closer together as a couple and make it more likely that you can overcome any standoffs you might have had otherwise. Talking good. Secrets bad. Lies worse. So, let's get started with the *How to Keep Your Marriage from Sucking* Engagement Quiz. Bon appétit!

ENGAGEMENT QUIZ

FINANCES

The money I make is considered...

A. Our money because we two are one, and I want to share everything with you.

B. My money. Keep your grubby paws off it you big free-loader. Get your own J-O-B.

C. I suppose it's our money since we're going to be married, but I might not want to put it all in the joint account because I'm not all that confident you know how to live within a budget. Maybe I'll have a separate account on the side and just put a portion of my money (I mean OUR money) in that account each month, so if you totally blow it, I won't completely panic.

D. I make money?

I know the state of my finances...

A. Always down to the penny.

B. On payday.

C. Once a year at tax time.

D. When the collections agencies call.

SPENDING

I would describe my spending habits as...

A. Impulsive. I can't leave the checkout line without getting suckered into a pack of gum, and, if I really love something, I get it in two colors. I live on the edge of my finances.

B. Cautious. I'm good at stretching a dollar and saving one. I live below my finances.

C. Reasonable. I spend money on quality not quantity and live well within my finances.

D. Out of control and I want to change...last week I bought a monkey.

I want to be able to spend money...

A. Whenever I want without having to check with you.

B. When it's important for the both of us.

C. On things we need for everyday life at my own discretion but check with you on big-ticket items.

D. To online shop like a motherfucker and hide my purchases from you, but please love me anyway.

For our first few newlywed years I would like to...

A. Live large now and then rein it in before we have kids.

B. Save for the future starting now and be responsible.

C. Travel and vacation as much as possible before we are shackled to real responsibilities.

D. Start our own zoo with that monkey I bought.

Where will we live? I would like to see us...

A. Buying a home ASAP and becoming homeowners.

B. Renting for the first few years until we can save up to buy.

C. Living in one of the dwellings we currently are in.

D. Staying with one of our parents to save money until it becomes awkward for everyone.

When I think of kids I see us...

A. Having an allergic reaction to the thought of them.

B. Wanting only one child because I loved being an only child.

C. Having at least two because I hate "only children."

D. Shooting the moon with three or more because I like a full house and want to make sure there's someone to look after us when *you're* in adult diapers.

Religious matters...

A. Not at all to me—religion is no biggie.

B. To my parents so we're going to have to pretend—I'm conveniently religious.

C. Did I mention that I want you to convert?

D. My religion is a huge part of my life and who I am, and that's not going to change no matter how hot you are.

Religion and kids...

A. Kids must be raised in the faith.

B. Can they be disciples of Yeezus?

C. If it's important to you, I'll pretend it's important to me.

D. I don't want religion to play a role in the way we raise our kids.

Families (in-laws)...

A. I'm marrying you, not your family, so keep them away from me.

B. My mother is the most important person to ever draw breath, and I will always choose her over you (but I don't want to have sex with her).

C. Big families are what make the world go around; the more the merrier.

D. I accept your family, warts and all because I love you...but we may end up drinking a lot.

E. Do we have to let our families know we're getting married?

Friends...

A. Your friends are great, and they get along with my friends. No lines being drawn here.

B. Here's the thing...you could do better. I think you should spend more time with my friends.

C. We each get to keep two, the rest are negotiable.

D. There is going to be a massive editing of friends. Players are getting cut from both teams in a bloodbath.

Careers...

A. We both have careers that are equally important.

B. Whoever makes the most money is the priority career.

C. I never said I wanted to be a stay-at-home mom.

D. Your band is a hobby, get a job.

E. You knew this was my life when you married me, so don't act surprised now.

Long-term goals...

A. To have kids and send them to college, vacation from time to time, and retire with money to move to Hawaii to raise chickens and bees.

B. To have no kids, travel whenever and wherever we want, and spend our lives together.

C. To get you elected to the Senate.

D. To find a way to be happy, no matter where life takes us, and be the envy of all our neighbors.

E. To get a reality series where we look like idiots but can release our own clothing line.

When we combine our things, we'll keep...

A. All my stuff only.

B. All your stuff only.

C. A little of this, a little of that—start fresh combining some of our stuff but also adding new stuff we choose together.

D. Just those pictures of you and your nana up at the lake.

E. Don't even think for a minute that your _____ is coming in this house.

DAILY LIFE

Who will do the household chores?

A. We will split them 50/50 and make a kick-ass Raise the Roof/Clean the House playlist and blast it while we clean our love palace.

B. Whoever loses the coin toss that week.

C. The housekeeper that we will gladly pay cold hard cash to.

D. I thought it was your turn.

E. Where do we keep the washer and dryer?

How will food happen?

A. I'll do the grocery shopping, you do the cooking.

B. We alternate grocery shopping and cooking depending on who has the time to do it.

C. I will orchestrate a complex and detailed schedule of weekly runs to Whole Foods, Trader Joe's, and the Farmer's Market and blow your mind with my wine pairings.

D. I only know how to make takeout.

E. I'll trade sexual favors to not have to cook, grocery shop, or think of food.

I'd like to eat dinner...

A. With you every night by 7 p.m. and talk about our respective days around the dinner table.

B. With you every night no later than 8:30 p.m., time and place TBD.

C. In front of the TV with my fingers while you're still at work.

D. With my friends at a restaurant, but I'll bring you takeout.

E. Every man for himself.

Sleep matters...

A. I'm an early riser but will bring you coffee in bed.

B. I'm a night owl and will make you stay up with me binge-watching Netflix because you love me...and I know your weak points.

C. Cuddling is something they made up in the movies— don't touch me while I sleep.

D. I will hog the covers like a baller and leave you shivering in your pajamas.

E. You'll have to work around my dog because he was here before you were.

If I'm sick...

A. Leave me the fuck alone.
B. Treat me like I'm seven and bring me grilled cheese, tomato soup, and ginger ale in bed.
C. Crawl into bed with me and get sick too so we can catch up on *House of Cards*.
D. Acknowledge that it sucks and buy me a present before abandoning me to save yourself.
E. I expect a stack of my favorite magazines and foods on my bedside table and for you to have queued up my favorite movies on the DVR.

AND FINALLY...

We should have a frank and open conversation about sex because...

A. We are best friends and should never be afraid to share who we are with each other no matter how embarrassing it may be because I am your safe place.
B. We are the only people we are supposed to have sex with for the rest of our lives.
C. I need to know what to get you for your birthday.
D. If we don't it could lead to problems down the road that have a devastating effect on our marriage...and no one wants that.
E. That shit is real.

The truth about me is that I like porn...

A. More than you know.

B. More than anyone you've ever met.

C. Not at all.

D. Occasionally when paired with the right wine.

E. Less than I like extensive dental surgery.

If you're into porn it will make me feel...

A. Like you're a healthy human being in touch with their sexuality.

B. Like you're a creep.

C. Like you'll expect our sex life to be off the charts and crazy all the time.

D. Like I'm never going to be enough to satisfy you.

E. Less than sexy, unless you at least share or explain why you like it so I can get a better grasp on it and you. And maybe we can try it together rather than you alone.

As far as our sex life goes...

A. I'm game for anything, anytime, anywhere.

B. I like to go the more traditional route—indoors mostly, no kink.

C. *50 Shades of Grey* is my bible.

D. I'd like to have one.

E. No animals watching.

F. No animals.

My libido is directly proportional to...

A. Our connection.

B. Your hotness.

C. Your paycheck.

D. My security in the relationship.

E. The testosterone that courses through my body.

5

wedding truths

ANY LITTLE GIRLS PLAY wedding from a very young age. They dress up their dolls as the bride and groom and hold weddings between their stuffed animals. They construct glorious gowns of tulle and chiffon, fashion a veil out of a scarf, and carry a bouquet of colored markers and imagine they are beautiful princess brides. The idea of getting married is total #lifegoals, even when we've only been on the planet for five years and have a bedtime of 7 p.m.

Weddings are a *thing*. Being a bride is an *even bigger thing*. Seriously. The idea that we get to be the architect of our own perfect dream wedding is such a life-defining experience that some spend the next twenty to thirty years thinking about it. Thinking about the dress alone could keep a girl busy for years. Think about how many times a woman might change her clothes to find the right outfit to have a low-key dinner with friends. Now multiply that by ten million. Dress options are endless and range from dream-worthy to God-awful. There are highly rated television shows dedicated to the process of picking out a wedding dress. Women will binge-watch complete strangers trying on wedding dresses because that's how fucking awesome wedding dresses are. For many, the wedding dress is the zenith of her life in fashion—the most important and memorable piece of clothing she'll wear in her lifetime. On a woman's deathbed, she won't remember what she wore home from the hospital after the birth of her first child or what she wore to the interview of her dream job, but she will be able to describe what she wore at her wedding in intricate detail.

Then there's the accessories. The veil takes the wedding dress from being a dress to being a MOMENT. The jewelry is of utmost importance; it must *complement* but not *overpower* the dress or veil. And the bouquet sets the tone for the colors of the bridal party, reception, invitations—everything! Hair up? Hair down? Half up, half down? Loose, beachy curls? Complicated yet stunning braid? There are sleepless nights debating the hairstyle.

Every piece of the wedding execution is weighted with such extreme importance that one wrong step can result in the dream day no longer being anything but a B-plus. That's how much pressure some women put on themselves and their wedding day.

So it's good to know going into wedding planning that this massive life event can make people crazy. It's not your fault if you go bananas or have completely irrational moments during the planning of your wedding. It's part of the process. We're here to help you decide what's worth getting crazy about, what has no lasting value, and things that other people won't tell you about the stage in your relationship that will always be defined by "The Wedding."

• • • •

THE SEVEN STAGES OF WEDDING PLANNING

Planning the wedding is like the inverse of the seven stages of grief. The stages are similar because both work as a huge appetite suppressant, but the feelings are more of elation, anxiety, and anticipation instead of gut-wrenching sadness. Basically, you're sick to your stomach but for totally different reasons.

STAGE 1: *shock or disbelief*

You can't believe this is happening. You've known it was coming, thought about it incessantly at times, dreamt of it, and obsessed about it, yet you still can't believe that it's actually happening.

STAGE 2: *denial*

Overwhelming thoughts settle in: This is impossible. There's just too much to plan, too much to do. There's no way in hell that we can pull this thing off. What were we thinking?

STAGE 3: *anger*

Why the hell is there so much to fucking plan? Why is your family so big? Seriously, how many cousins do you have? Why didn't we just decide to elope? Picking between these four shades of Tiffany Blue makes me want to pull your eyes out. Planning this wedding is the same as being waterboarded.

STAGE 4: *bargaining*

If I do tables of twelve instead of tables of ten then I can cut down the number of table rentals and the number of center-pieces and put the money from the extra table rentals and centerpieces toward my dress.

STAGE 5: *guilt*

This is costing my parents/his parents/us more than an annual mortgage. Is this really what we should spend this money on? It could be the down payment on a house. What are we doing? Who are we right now to think that it's okay to ask someone to cough up that much money so that we can stand in front of a bunch of people in fancy outfits?

STAGE 6: *depression*

What is wrong with me? Do I really need to have these things to love my wedding? Am I really that shallow? Will the extra flute player make my walk down the aisle that much better? Does the more expensive DJ guarantee my marriage will be happier?

STAGE 7: *acceptance and hope*

Okay, we're going to just power through this. We can do this. We just need to make a little dent in it every day. If we make a few compromises, redo the budget, put the money where it really makes a difference, it will all work out. It might even be fun.

• • • •

BE FOREWARNED

There will be a night, many years after you are married, where you will throw the perfect party. It probably will be thrown together at the last minute or it was someone's 43rd and not their 50th, or whatever, but it will be the perfect combination of guests, the food will be magical, someone will bring an unexpected desert, the shuffle in your iWhatever will keep getting it right, conversation will flow like a river, and it will go far later than you expected. And here's the weirdest part: even though you threw the fucking thing, YOU also had a great time.

Your wedding will not be like this. A party, no matter how formal, should always have an air of being casual. That's why it's a party. A wedding, however, is a show. Got that? A wedding is a show dressed up as a party—but it is a show. It must be directed, costumed, and stage-managed like a show. There's a curtain time and a closing number. Then, maybe after all is said and done, there is a little after party.

We're not being cynical. If anything, we're trying to set you up to understand the event better and, in the end, make it more enjoyable for you. If you look at it like a show, with all its various acts and set pieces, you might be able to get a handle on it better.

Think of it like this: You and your mate have been cast as the two most in love people in the whole world and today the whole world is going to watch you make that official. First you will have to decide where this awesome event will take place. Where will we stage our show? St. Anthony's Cathedral? A beach in Mexico? Your friend's backyard? Your friends and family will be playing the part of "the chorus." How big do you want that chorus to be? Remember you get to create the ideal world for your show, so only put the people in your chorus that make that world special; do not cast people just to fill seats or that you don't like. It's your show, you don't have to have villains in it.

You can create as much or as little drama in your wedding show as you see fit. Remember, you are the writer/producer/director, and, as such, you make the hard decisions. So what if the Kendersons have been your dad's colleagues since you were a baby? Do you know them? Do they really matter as much as some of your friends from work? Remember what your show is about and who the central characters are in it.

The ceremony is the climax of the whole thing. Sometimes religion dictates how this takes place; other times you can create a ceremony to your own liking. Regardless, remember that what you say to each other at the ceremony is most important. The biggest moment is the one where you devote yourselves to one another. We all came to see you fall in love more deeply. We all came for your Happily Ever After. We all want to be a part of that moment where we as a group say I do. So really concentrate on this part because, by this moment, the dress will be seen, the invitations will be in the trash, and the Kendersons will have already missed their flight. While this moment is happening, you will suddenly realize *this is all anyone cares about.*

A NOTE FROM GREG

THIS PAST SUMMER, I officiated my first wedding. I loved it and since then have been asked to do more. I met with the couple to find out how they wanted "the show" to go down. They asked if I'd keep it light and quick but gave me permission to be as funny as I wanted. They also said I could use any "language" (meaning curse words) I wanted, as there would be a lot of stand-up fans there.

I wrote a funny monologue to open the ceremony with and figured the couple would read their vows right afterward. I was pleased with what I had written. But the day before their wedding, I heard an interview with the actress Lake Bell, who had been married by actor/comedian Rob Cordry. The host of the interview said, "Oh that must have been hilarious," and Lake Bell replied, "No, in fact, it had been quite beautiful."

I got to thinking about this moment, the centerpiece of the whole show. I realized it wasn't about me being funny. I was happy to keep it light, but I also wanted to respect the moment and share a bit about why marriage is important to me. I trimmed some of the language and added an anecdote about how marriage is about who you want to be with when your ship hits the rocks. I spoke about how I'd been diagnosed with cancer this past year, and, when I woke from surgery, my wife was the first person I saw—and the only person in the world I always want to see.

I shared something real because I believe in what it was these two people were doing. I believe in marriage, and I love marriage. The couple read their touching vows to each other, and in the bride's vows, she said the reason she wanted to be with her groom was because he had visited her every day in the hospital when she was sick. It was a story I didn't know. The whole assembly was in tears, including me, watching and experiencing profound love. It's why we all wore suits in 102°F weather in a large grassy backyard—so we could watch and experience profound love...

And, finally, there is that last act: The reception—the giant party that you have thrown not for you but for your guests. This is a grand thank you to the people you love the most. There will be toasts to you, but the food, the band, and the open bar is for them. If you think of it as a production you are putting on for others' enjoyment, you will have a much better time. Far better than if you are trying to put on the "Most Important Day of Your Life Party."

THE TWO SIDES OF THE COIN

the upside of doing it right...

Pulling off a kick-ass wedding is something that no one can ever take away from you as a couple. It is proof positive that, when you come together, you are an undeniable force that is capable of incredible magic. It seals your fate as a powerful team.

the downside of doing it right...

Your friends will compare their weddings to yours and theirs won't stack up, which will make you feel badly for them while also feeling secretly superior. Also, when marriage gets rough—and believe us, things do get rough—it will feel extra sucky because your life together started out so charmed.

the upside of doing it wrong...

You can always renew your vows down the road on your fifth, tenth, whatever number anniversary, and throw yourself an amazing do-over wedding and have an incredible second act as a couple.

the downside of doing it wrong...

It's possible that you've just set the tone for a truly disappointing chapter in your lives that you'll look back on as the "Can you believe I actually married that person? I should have known from the wedding that it was going to be a disaster" period of your life.

• • • •

HOW WE FAILED AND SUCCEEDED IN THE PLANNING AND EXECUTION OF OUR WEDDING

The Lead-Up: Greg's Story

What I liked about being engaged was simple: Amiira Ruotola was a catch! She was an outright bombshell: brown eyes, legs for days, the world's best laugh. She was an "Oh my God, that's your fiancé?" type of girl, and so for very real and for very shallow reasons I loved being engaged to my soon-to-be wife.

And I brought Amiira anywhere could. I was very proud that she had said yes to me, and I was very proud to show her off. I wanted people to see and know what I had done. To me Amiira was like a Harvard Law Degree—a thing to brag about to impress almost everyone, especially the ones who thought it was out of your league.

Being engaged also gave me a sense of purpose I'd not had in a relationship before. It was as though I'd been brought up to the major leagues from AAA ball and was in spring training. It was happening. Bonding myself to Amiira gave me the kind of super power I didn't feel again until we had our firstborn. Maybe it's all the hope or the potential of what is about to come. It's like Christmas Eve versus Christmas Day. It's not knowing what's ahead but believing it's going to be magical. Your engagement can be one of the greatest times of your life and certainly your relationship.

Here's the thing: I wanted a wedding. A *wedding* wedding with all the trimmings: best man, groomsmen, bridesmaids, proper morning jackets, rehearsal dinner, speeches, toasts, bride's family on one side, groom's on the other, people throwing rice or flowers petals, a killer reception, an amazing brass band, and a big-ass cake. That's what I had dreamt about but it's not at all what Amiira had.

Suddenly, the details started to fall into place in my head. We'd have the wedding on a beach in Hawaii, where Amiira's family lived. My four best friends, my parents, and my sister would fly out. The wedding itself would be blissfully simple. Vintage aloha shirts for the grooms, my dad as my best man. I'd forgo the tux rental in lieu of us all renting surfboards the next day at the north shore and making asses out of ourselves. Amiira would look like she always does at the beach—like some ethereal sea goddess. She might even be half naked or wearing clam shells—who knows? She'd be perfection. The reception would be ten feet from where the wedding took place, on the beach, and the band would play everything—but they would ask me to join them on a version of Dick Dale's *The Wedge*, which, BTDUBS, I nail.

It was a perfect wedding scenario in my head because I picked the perfect wife.

I told Amiira my idea and we were both excited—and then it didn't happen the way I dreamt it. At all.

The Lead-Up: Amiira's Story

When I was young, I used to proclaim quite confidently that I was going to be married three times. That, to me, seemed ideal. The idea of having three great loves of my life and spending just part of my life with each of them sounded right to me. I never could see myself with only one person for my entire adult life or only getting to have those great marquee relationship moments only once in my life. I wanted more than one wedding, and, at the same time, I wanted no weddings. Instead, I wanted to have small "quasi weddings" with each of my three grooms, but no big church weddings or highly attended weddings that involved me being the center of attention.

I'm good in social situations with a handful of people. I'm also very independent, so I liked the idea of having some down time between relationships where I'm not responsible for or to another human being all the time. I didn't dream about always being in a relationship. In fact, I always liked being single when I was single. This is probably because it was a temporary, not eternal, state. I'd probably feel differently about liking being single if I didn't get to break up the monotony of being single with some romantic relationships and companionship. Being single can get lonely just like being married can get lonely. The grass is always greener, right?

In my younger me fantasy, I also had great plans for the marriages, like living in different countries and exotic locales with each of my three husbands. I envisioned my first wedding as some sort of sweep-me-off-my-feet impulsive set of "I do's" at the top of the Eiffel Tower or some beautiful and old English landmark. It would be a spur-of-the-moment, on-the-run type of deal that had no planning other than needing to find someone to marry us and calling our families after the fact to tell them that we had gotten hitched...which explains my first wedding. It had a similar blueprint but without the overseas travel. It was us, five friends, and an Elvis impersonator in Vegas, a spur-of-the-moment super-fun wedding with little to no evidence of it two-plus decades later. Perfect and nearly untraceable—unless you're my parents who didn't love being excluded from their only daughter's wedding.

I saw the second wedding happening barefoot on a beach somewhere beautiful and tropical with just immediate family and a few friends. I don't even think I thought I'd be wearing a dress, maybe just a bikini—probably not even a white one—and some flowers in my hair. It, too, would require little to no planning, other than finding someone to marry us and telling our closest peeps which beach and when—no frills, no fuss. This could have easily been Greg's and my wedding had there not been factors which swayed us in another direction.

My third wedding would probably be on some sort of a yacht, and then we'd sail away somewhere posh afterwards for our honeymoon because, by this point in my life, I would be falling for rich guys with yachts, not young, funny, and broke guys.

Looking back, it's clear to me that I never wanted to plan a wedding or really be at the center of a wedding. I wanted to be in love and married, but the wedding wasn't the important part. Don't get me wrong. I love wearing beautiful things and eating incredible food in the company of people I adore, but I didn't connect those things with me getting married.

Weddings resonate differently with different people. Some women wait their whole life for the opportunity to plan their wedding, and others break into hives at the thought. I was always somewhere in the middle but leaning slightly more toward the hives end of the scale. When I look back at both of my weddings, I see them with tremendous joy and know they were both quite lovely reflections of the relationships they represent and who we were at that moment of time in our lives. Neither of my weddings was perfect, but perfection is not something that I was aiming for. I was shooting for meaningful, memorable, and fun...and no family members in tears that would later turn into resentments. I was partially successful on all counts both times. (Again, sorry Mom and Dad about that first one.)

Being untraditional can mean a million things when it comes to the framework of a wedding. The most important thing is that you try to remain sane and true to yourself and your fiancé during the mental and emotional obstacle course that is wedding planning.

• • • •

HOW OUR WEDDING CAME TO BE

When we first started to volley some ideas back and forth about our wedding, it quickly became clear that we were not really on the same page with our desires for that special day. Greg wanted an elaborate church wedding that looked like a scene from a Richard Curtis movie, with the groomsmen in morning jackets (and possibly even top hats), and a gigantic processional of pageantry. Something cinematic. Amiira wanted to be outside on a remote beach and have only her six favorite people included, but a destination wedding wasn't going to be in the cards due to family health concerns. Our attempts to compromise consisted of each of us offering an idea and the other softly smothering it to death.

> **GREG:** How about Grace Cathedral in San Francisco? It's old and beautiful...
>
> **AMIIRA:** ...I can't really picture getting married in a cathedral having only been in a church a handful of times in my life. What about somewhere downtown?

GREG: Downtown L.A.? Why? That holds no value to us as a couple. We've barely ever been to downtown L.A. together...

AMIIRA: But there are hotels with rooftop restaurants that have a view of the L.A. skyline...

GREG: Something that we've never even seen together and means nothing to us.

AMIIRA: Neither is the view from Grace Cathedral.

GREG: Okay...what about the beach. We both love the beach...

AMIIRA: We love the beach in Hawaii, not the beach in Southern California, which we've never gone to together.

GREG: So we do it in Hawaii.

AMIIRA: Then your mom and grandma probably wouldn't be able to come. Your mom will still be in treatment and have a compromised immune system, and your grandma won't travel by air anymore.

GREG: So, basically, Malibu, Zuma, Laguna...all places we've never gone...

AMIIRA: ...and have no connection to us.

GREG: What about just a hotel in Beverly Hills or Hollywood?

AMIIRA: Do you want to watch a movie?

GREG: Can I nap during it?

AMIIRA: Hell yeah. Wedding planning makes me tired. What movie should we nap to?

GREG: *Four Weddings and a Funeral*?

Amiira here to confess something. When I say that wedding planning makes me tired, a more accurate statement would be that it makes me narcoleptic. I literally cannot stay awake during wedding talk. I think it's my body's natural defenses trying to protect me from conflict. Even though planning a wedding is as awesome as it is stressful, I still would feel my eyelids drooping to half-mast and my head falling slowly forward, then jerking suddenly awake again. My brain just could not focus or lock onto what was being discussed.

We couldn't really agree on anything enthusiastically. There were a lot of, "I guess that would be okay," "It's not really what I would want but I can live with it," and, "We can't because of..." Whenever we tried to get liftoff on an idea we just couldn't get it off the ground. We knew we wanted to get married but planning the wedding was becoming a chore instead of a joy. There was no real right type of wedding for us that we could agree on or even feel excited by. Our families were also weighing in, and we couldn't get all the parties to agree on things that we needed them to agree on OR maybe we just assumed they wouldn't agree because we didn't ask. That's also a possibility in retrospect.

It's weird the way your balloon can get deflated when your wedding suggestions get shot down. That low-grade stress that amplifies every possible choice and makes things seem bigger than they are. It seemed like we were going to end up with a wedding that didn't resonate deeply with either of us until we came up with the idea that rocked us both.

• • • •

GREG AND AMIIRA'S SUPER EXCELLENT SURPRISE WEDDING

When we couldn't figure out a wedding that made us both happy, we came up with the idea of taking over a restaurant that we loved and having a big "Engagement Party," then surprising all the guests by getting married. While throwing a party and throwing a wedding have some similarities, there is less to plan, fewer moving parts to deal with. We had no wedding party, so there was no need to find tuxedos and gowns that flattered all shapes and sizes. Flowers were easy peasy because the restaurant already covered centerpieces for all the tables; we just had to order a bridal bouquet, a boutonniere for the groom, and a couple of floral head wreaths for Amiira's cousins that had been promised to be flower girls and felt ripped off by the lack of a formal wedding.

There was no staff to hire and no rentals to deal with because the restaurant had all those things. The menu we chose was done in courses that were our favorite dishes from the restaurant's preexisting menu. All we needed to do was hire a DJ, pick a wedding cake (its own glorious undertaking), and find someone to marry us. We had our friend, Chris Bilheimer (the stunningly talented art designer who did the cover art to this and our previous books), create an invitation for our "Engagement Party." We asked our friend, Joey Seehee (a roller-skating lounge singer and former Jesuit priest) to marry us because we had been to another wedding that he presided over, and it was fantastic. A coworker took the wedding video, and everyone wore what they wanted to, including us.

The party started around 6 p.m. on a Saturday night in August. The restaurant was an old California Craftsman house with a shark sticking out of the roof. It had a big outside patio area where waiters passed cocktails, and we greeted all our guests. Everyone mingled and chatted for about an hour during which we snuck upstairs to get ready. Amiira changed from her cocktail dress into her wedding dress, and Greg added a tie and boutonniere to his already dapper suit. Once changed, our friend, Eric, announced to the crowd that we had something very special that we wanted to share with everyone. As Greg came downstairs and made his way to the front of the restaurant and the dub version of "Ave Maria" began to play there was first a hush followed by a hum of excitement that swept through the restaurant. Then Amiira descended the stairs on her father's arm, wearing a gown and holding a bouquet. People freaked out when they realized what was happening.

As the couple doing the surprising, it was exhilarating to have pulled off a surprise wedding. The energy in the air was that of complete giddiness and glee. Our siblings stood up for us along with Amiira's flower girl cousins, and our respective best friends from childhood, who we had let in on the secret, each did a reading. Our service was uniquely weird, cool, and touching.

Joey managed to compare marriage to the movie *The Insider* (about big tobacco using the concept of "delivery systems"—a cigarette for tobacco and a marriage for love) which was funny and weird, just like us. We each wrote our own vows and we exchanged rings. When we were proclaimed officially married by Joey and had our first married kiss, the crowd erupted in applause and hollers.

Our wedding was magical and completely unique. We completely skirted any wedding expectations that anyone may have had (including ourselves) and knocked it out of the park. It was like having breakfast for dinner—something so simple that feels completely surprising because it's out of context. Our guests danced and dined. Our cake was an explosion of catawampus cakes and colors that recalled *Alice in Wonderland*. After everyone went home, we gathered the uneaten meals, and a friend drove them to the local shelter. We collected all our belongings and headed out to Malibu to Shutters by The Beach, where our room was filled with champagne and rose petals. It was simple, surprising, and perfectly us.

WEDDING INSANITY QUOTE #1

"Getting married is a near-death experience. While you're standing there and the priest is talking, all you hear is white noise, and you see your entire life flash before your eyes. But then, instead of dying, you have to spend the rest of your life with one person. A few years into marriage, I realized that death might have been preferable."

—Kristen Behrendt
(in reference to her own marriage)

the ultimate wedding planning guide from the couple who couldn't plan their own wedding

IKE WE TALKED ABOUT earlier, in the movie of your life there are Trailer Moments, and getting married is a major Trailer Moment. But making it happen can make you stressed out, anxious, and possibly unsure of your ability to speak words until you get through the ceremony. The wedding—the Trailer Moment—is the culmination of hundreds of hours of thought and effort and thousands of dollars spent. And though it's too late to change anything, you won't be able to stop yourself from obsessing over something that you've suddenly changed your mind about and wish you had done differently. It's part of the Wedding Insanity that we all succumb to when we've put such a tremendous amount of pressure on ourselves to make everything perfect. Just know going into it that it's going to be great. Truly. It will be because *you have the perfect taste for you,* and no one will even remember anything besides the wedding dress, unless someone falls and breaks a hip or throws up on the cake.

Plan your wedding with the intention that it's really for you and your favorite person of all time, above all others. You will be the one that thinks about it repeatedly after it's done, not your new mother-in-law or your sixth bridesmaid. This is your chance to give yourself incredible memories. And you know you better than anybody else—don't get strong armed into doing anything that doesn't feel right.

The first thing that you need to decide is what kind of wedding you want to have. We've been to weddings of all varieties. Some have had themes, like modern vintage; some have been formal Catholic church weddings; and some had just a handful of people in attendance on a beach. But all have reflected the couple getting hitched.

Your wedding gets to be what you make of it. If your dream is to exchange vows on a cliff overlooking the ocean at dusk with the trees illuminated with white twinkle lights, followed by a casual affair with food trucks, then do it. Own it and do it for the two of you. (Also, if you're having food trucks at your wedding, can we please be invited?)

There are a lot of moving pieces that you need to land for a kick-ass wedding. And all of these things need to fit within a budget that you can all live comfortably with. Most weddings cost a pretty penny, so you have frank conversations up front about where you want to splurge and where you want to skimp. Whose money are you spending? If it's your own, you will certainly spend it differently than if it's someone else's, but we'll get to that a bit later.

Start a wedding binder to keep things organized. To start your planning, try out this exercise. *Think of all the weddings that you've been to. What are the elements that stood out to you and your partner the most? (These might be very different things.)*

Do you remember what the invitation looked like?

What was special about the location?

What about the centerpieces at the reception?

The bridal bouquet?

Decorations at the ceremony?

The reception?

What did you eat?

Was there a band?

What was your favorite thing about it?

Was there any day before or after wedding activities that you really loved?

Write down your favorite answers for the questions above. Other people's weddings are a great starting point to find out what you want most in your own. Once you have a personal barometer of "oohs and aahs," then you can start plotting for your big day.

Remember, hidden in each of the moving parts we outlined earlier are hidden costs. Let us give you an example.

Invitations/Stationery:

Obvious costs:

▶ standard printing and design fees

Hidden costs:

▶ printing costs for extra communications, such as save-the-date cards, reply cards, information cards for out-of-towners, menu and place cards, etc.

- added printing costs for fancy details, like lined envelopes
- postage costs for invitations and reply cards
- calligrapher fees

It always ends up being more than you thought. There are hidden costs everywhere when planning a wedding because there's more than meets the eye or the brain. Unless you happen to be a professional wedding planner yourself, there will be many surprises. The great news is this will teach you and your person how to negotiate with each other, prioritize, and compromise. It's like a microcosm of marriage and an obstacle course all rolled up into one. If you can plan a wedding and still want to marry the person, then you are slaying the game. Go you!

● ● ● ●

WHAT'S REALLY IMPORTANT?

In your life together as a couple, you will constantly come up against the task of deciding what is important versus what seems important but really isn't. Planning your wedding is a grand trial by fire into this foray as a unit, so remember: you are a team first and foremost. All the trappings and pageantry are just stuff at the end of the day. The important thing is the future you will have together from your wedding day onward.

What are the most important things on your wedding day? We think it's to love how you look, to love where you're getting married and having the reception, to feel stress-free about the guest list, and to have incredible photos to look back on. Now you make your own list. If you are a super foodie couple, maybe it's the catering, wine pairings, and cake that you prioritize. If you live for art direction and design, maybe you throw your budget behind the theme and decorations. It's your big day and your budget to allocate as you see fit as a couple.

There are sneaky ways to cut back and stretch your dollars, so cut away whenever you can so that you can spend your money on the good stuff. Even the closest couples don't always feel strongly about the same aspects of the wedding planning or understand why something in particular is so important to their mate. It's a give and take in the truest sense, so negotiation and reallocation of funds is imperative for both of you to get what you want and need from your wedding day. You don't want to look back at your wedding and wish you had spent the money on another hour of the band playing at the reception instead of the live butterfly release as you left the chapel where half of the butterflies didn't even fly out of their little origami boxes.

● ● ● ●

CUTTHROAT GUEST LIST

The guest list is where things can get prickly between the bride, the groom, and the respective families. There are guests that are a must, guests that are a want, and guests that are an obligation. Some families are bigger than others, some families are closer than others, and some families are more difficult than others. Couples usually go through a few rough patches when it comes to the guest list.

The price of the wedding is usually determined by the size of the guest list. There are fixed costs in a wedding budget, and while the venue itself may be fixed, the number of tables, meals, and booze are headcount-specific. Every time you add a table to the reception you add not only that many meals to the mix but also the rental costs of table and chairs, linens, flatware, silverware, glassware, centerpiece/decorations, and possibly more serving staff to serve that table. Every domino leans on another and adds up to money spent, sometimes substantially so.

Decide on the size of wedding you want upfront. There's no magic wand you can wave to make this part of wedding planning easy because, undoubtedly, there will be people who you feel you should invite but don't want to or those you can't invite but want to because the budget is already high. The guest list struggle is real.

To start, make a list of absolutely everyone you'd like to invite, think you should invite, and must invite. It may be a very long list with second cousins that you've only seen on Facebook in the last decade and people from work that are only work friends. Put everyone on because you will most likely add and subtract names in the coming weeks until you land on the perfect guest list for your budget.

To do this math, delineate family, family friends, bride friends, groom friends, couple friends, people whose wedding you have been invited to, and strangers that your parents said you had to invite, and start making the hard decisions. Immediate family and close-but-extended families are musts. Wedding party people are musts. After that, it becomes negotiable. With "musts" alone you could already be at fifty guests or more.

Next, create a system to begin fine-tuning the list. One way is for each of you to pick your top ten wedding guests. Or top twenty. Another way is to take turns crossing a name off the list. It's like playing the wedding version of "If you could only save one person from a fire, who would it be? Becca or Jamie?" Only this is less gruesome. But sometimes you have to throw two wedding guest names into a cage match and see who comes out the victor.

Let's start a master list:

Bride's immediate family (mother, father, siblings)

Bride's extended family (grandparents, aunts, uncles, cousins)

Bridesmaids (assuming this covers very best friends)

Groom's immediate family (mother, father, siblings)

Groom's extended family (grandparents, aunts, uncles, cousins)

Groomsmen (assuming this covers very best friends)

Bride's closest family friends (honorary aunts, uncles, and families)

Groom's closest family friends (honorary aunts, uncles, and families)

Bride's must haves (close friends)

Groom's must haves (close friends)

How many guests are you up to so far? Does it feel small and intimate? Could you be happy with this being the final list? If yes, then hallelujah! If the answer is no, then it's time to put the guest list through the wedding invitation ringer to get to your final count. Here are some questions to help you with the weeding out:

▶ Are either of you related to this person, even distantly?
▶ Will it create family drama if they are not invited?
▶ Do either of you work or go to school with this person?

▶ Do you regularly spend time with this person besides at school or work?

▶ Have you seen or spoken to this person anytime in the past year, besides on social media or through text message?

▶ Were you invited to their wedding?

▶ Have either of you talked about the wedding with this person?

▶ Would this person's presence make your wedding better or more fun?

▶ Can this person stay up late enough to see the cutting of the cake?

▶ Could you just as easily have brunch with them after the honeymoon to make up for not inviting them?

▶ Is it worth $100 or more to either of you to have this person at your wedding?

▶ Will you regret it deeply if you don't invite this person?

After answering these questions, you should be able to cross several names off the guest list.

Finalizing the guest list to your wedding is agonizing, but just know that every married couple that has gone before you has been there too, and they feel your pain. Surely everyone you know would love to go to your wedding because you are awesome and so are weddings. But also, surely everyone you know would understand if they weren't invited. Excluding family and BFFs, it's absolutely okay to just say, "If money were no object I'd invite you to come, but that's not the case, and we had to scale back on the guest list significantly. I'm so sorry." Chances are that you will be pleased by the uninvited person's response to such honesty. No one thinks weddings are free, so don't beat yourself up if you can't invite everyone. Half of the time when we receive a wedding invitation we are completely surprised to have made the cut.

• • • •

HOW TO REGISTER
SO YOUR MARRIAGE DOESN'T FAIL

Registering for your wedding is one of the most delicious parts of your whole wedding experience. It's the beginning of you planning your new fantasy life as a couple with some choice new stuff. Registering for your wedding is a free pass to shop with other people's money. Do not waste this opportunity. You should really think it through, or you'll end up with a bunch of useless crap that takes up precious space in your home and a failed marriage. (Just kidding! There's really no correlation between wedding registries and divorce rates but that title made us laugh.)

Have a goal and a game plan. Don't just go into Bloomingdale's with the registry gun and think you know what you're doing. When we registered for our wedding, we did it mostly wrong because we didn't have a clear idea of our goal. Our issue was that we are both traditional enough to think that we needed to register for things that one traditionally registers for, upgrades included. After years of living on our own, we already owned everything we needed. So, basically, we registered for an upgrade of everyday kitchen stuff that was a nicer version of what we both already had. Then we registered for china. Twelve place settings of actual china, complete with matching serving dishes and stemware and flatware and linens. We registered for what would ultimately be the most elaborate dinner table that we use maybe twice a year, if we're the ones hosting Thanksgiving and Christmas.

Turns out, we are not fancy china people. We are more casual diners, even for the two big dinner holidays. We registered for a hand crank pasta maker and a mandolin to finely shred things on its dangerously sharp blades, a wok, and some other such nonsense, none of which we still own because neither of us has time in our lives to make pastas from scratch or julienne the ends of our fingers for some bullshit tarte that isn't ever as good as frozen tater tots anyway. Of course, if you're twenty-something and don't have good pots, pans, plates, and glasses, or any decent small appliances, then, by all means, go kitchen crazy.

Looking back, here's what we should have registered for: contributions toward a piece of art that we both really love that could hang in our house forever. Or travel contributions toward that honeymoon we never actually took.

Expand your registry horizons. There are practical registries, new home registries, honeymoon registries, you name it. If you can think of it, you can create it. Have a registry meeting and decide what your priority is. Consider this some preparation for all of those decision-making meetings you'll have as a married couple. If you are going on an incredible honeymoon, register for some great luggage. If you can't start your day without a trip to Starbucks, register for a top of the line coffee/espresso machine. Are you about to start construction on a fixer upper? Register for new bathroom tiles. What will jumpstart your life together? Is it a hundred lottery tickets? Register for that. Skip the deep fryer, rice cooker, and candy thermometer, and get the stuff that will be impactful in your life.

Get real about who you are and the most meaningful way for your wedding guests to contribute to your new married life. Be sure to offer many price points so that everyone can get you something they can comfortably afford and have fun with it. Better yet, if you have everything you could possibly need, skip registering altogether and ask your guests to make donations to your favorite charity.

Whatever it may be, do it together and have fun with it. If one of you got their way more in the planning of the wedding, let the other get theirs in the registry. Shopping with other people's money is super fun, and you rarely get to do it in your adult life.

WEDDING INSANITY QUOTE #2

"Once I got to the altar, I thought I was going to throw up. My mouth was dry, I felt light headed. My body was telling me that I didn't want to get married after all. But then I looked around and there were all these people who traveled to be there, and I figured that I had to, so I did."

—Sharon Ruotola
(Amiira's mother who just celebrated her 52nd anniversary with Amiira's father)

• • • •

WHAT I WISH I HAD KNOWN THEN
By Greg

When we started this book, I didn't know what it was about. I knew we were advocating that marriage could be great, even though at the time ours wasn't. We were, at the time, for reasons not even clear to us, unwilling to throw in the towel. In looking at our/my problems, I realized that so many of them were operating outside the marriage instead of inside the institution we created. Because we never did that. We never sat down and wrote out the bylaws and protections, the rules and regulations of this lifetime venture of loving one another. Yes, we wrote vows but they were mostly silly and what you'd expect two funny, smart people who are giddy in love would say. They were the only rules or promises we made to one another. And there were a lot of unspoken rules. Meaning things I just assumed were or were not going to happen that did and or didn't happen.

Here's how I would correct that. I believe marriage, like yoga, meditation, or running, is a practice. It is a sacred space shared by those that want to enter into it and as such should have rituals that honor it and keep it in tact. A marriage ceremony is an act of love. A fucking expensive one at that. Why do we say vows, or have a long kiss, be forced to make eye contact for longer than five minutes on just this one day? Your ceremony should be the largest version of a smaller practice you will try to do every day for the rest of your life to insure the safety of your union and everything that springs from it, children, homes, business, etc. Whatever the two of you create together or separately must not supplant or be used as an excuse to supplant the marriage. The marriage is always the thing that takes the hit, mostly because we've made it an empty container, a status, not a practice.

Many married people use the phrase "I can't, I'm married." For many reasons. But in that sentiment is the idea that I've put myself in a limiting institution. As opposed to saying, "I don't have to, I'm married." Which says I've found happiness, or contentment. I guess what I'm saying is your marriage ceremony and day should be the guide book to the new religion of your love. A practice you undertake every day in small ways always reminding you what is at stake.

it's about you
but not only you

ERE IS A PERSPECTIVE we didn't get until we had our own children. A marriage is the final nail in the "I don't need you anymore" coffin. Of course, we don't mean that as children being done with their parents. But let's be honest—in agreeing to marry, you have officially decided to put your love, trust, care, and well-being into the hands of another person, and that person is not your parents, or however many people spent their time raising you. So, know this: Both of your parents will be on edge.

Therefore, it is crucial that you give both families a wide berth during wedding season. *Especially the family that's footing the bill.* Change, no matter how great or beautiful, is always hard, so remember all their tension or unreasonable needs come from a place of not wanting to let you go yet—after all, you always will be their child. Or because they feel like they don't have some say in your life anymore. *(P.S. They always will a little bit.)* That said, this is also the beginning of your own family. Even if it's only the two of you, it's now become what your parents' family became—the most important relationship of your life. This is also the time when you politely claim your independence and start making decisions based on what's best for the both of you and how you'd like to see your wedding play out.

As a new couple, we walked that tightrope pretty well and have continued to do so throughout our marriage. We made concessions because of our families' various needs and health issues, but we still had the wedding we wanted. Neither of us was going to push anything that would make our wedding difficult or upset some familial balance. It wasn't worth it to us to push something through at the expense of something important.

We did us while also respecting our families, and, quite honestly, it set the tone for our life. From our unconventional career choices to our children's names, we welcomed Mom and Dad's input, but we ultimately did what we did and still do. Now, to be fair, we happen to have beautiful families on both sides. Greg's family can be a bit distant and Amiira's family will share a bed with you if you let them, but it works.

Wedding planning stress and decisions may amplify a family's challenging qualities. Things are very likely to get prickly between you and your family members. Everyone will just be in a heightened state of easily ignited agitation because of what the wedding means to them personally. Keep this in mind as you navigate the dynamics. There will be concessions that you must make for your fiancé's family or for your fiancé, so they don't have to go down the family drama rabbit hole and vice versa.

Your family won't be a dream to your fiancé, either. Being in the middle between the person you're marrying and your family is incredibly stressful and tough. The guilt will keep you up at night and put a pit in your stomach. It feels awful to disappoint your parents, and it feels terrible to choose them over your fiancé, but there will be times when you must upset one to please the other or yourself. There's no two ways around it when it comes to the sensitive issue of planning a wedding, but know this: Everyone will recover and be happy on your wedding day.

• • • •

DON'T BE *THAT* BRIDE

Amiira here. I have had the incredible privilege to be a bridesmaid several times in my life. It truly is one of the greatest moments in my friendships with each of the brides. There's the excitement of being in the inner circle for all the good stuff, like watching one of your best friends try on wedding gowns. Seeing that wave of incredulousness pass over her face when she sees herself for the first time wearing a wedding gown. I'll never forget that look or that moment. Planning the bridal shower and bachelorette party with the other bridesmaids like a total boss squad. It's so much fun to be part of crew whose only mission is to celebrate the friend that brought you all together. Sharing so many special moments with a person who holds a truly significant place in your heart. It's an incredible bonding experience that really isn't replicated in other expressions of friendship. This is one of the parts that I regret not having in my surprise wedding, but it would have wrecked the surprise if there just happened to be a handful of my besties all wearing the same color dress at our elopement party. I love the feeling of being lifted and supported by your best friends who usher you into marriage as much as whomever walks you down the aisle. To me it is a significant part of what is magical about the whole wedding experience.

You know when being a bridesmaid is not great? When your bride does not let the bridesmaids shine in their own way. When the bride loves a color that is amazing in actual nature on a flower but doesn't look amazing on any humans, or she loves a silhouette that accentuates your least favorite body parts. The makeup queen bride who doesn't go to SoulCycle without a fully done face is all about a natural dewy look—for her bridesmaids—but she herself is made up like a movie star.

I've been the bridesmaid to brides who didn't let their bridesmaids look or feel their best for the big day, and it's weird. You know each other so well, but she's the dictator of the day who gets to decide what you will look like. She makes a choice that delights her but puzzles her bridesmaids. For example, I was in a wedding once where the bride chose a hot pink, crinkle, shiny balloon gown (the skirt of the gown ballooned out from waist to ankle but then gathered tightly at the bottom underneath to look like an upside down hot air balloon). She also had us wear bouffant '50s hairstyles and Amy Winehouse makeup. The bride looked amazing, but we felt ridiculous. It honestly felt like a prank. Here's what I'll say about the bride today: It's not a friendship I fought to keep alive after we both had kids and got busy in our lives.

Another time I was a bridesmaid where the bridesmaids' gowns were stunning. Gorgeous color, beautiful style, the shoes and jewelry were on point. It was seemingly awesome. The bridesmaids all felt amazing getting dressed together. We were giddy with excitement. Then a stylist showed up as a surprise from the bride to do our hair and makeup. The stylist had a picture as a reference that the bride wanted her to recreate and—I kid you not—it was center-parted straight hair in a low ponytail and a completely neutral face with what appeared to be no eyeliner, mascara, or lip color. It was very editorial and would look impactful on a runway where all you want to see is the clothes, but to us bridesmaids, it was a pretty big blow. We were an attractive bunch of ladies, but it's not like we look collectively like Cara Delevingne, Kendall Jenner, Gigi Hadid, and Karlie Kloss with no makeup. None of us were winning any cheekbone or perfect brow awards anytime soon. It was such a letdown to be told that for all intents and purposes none of us could wear makeup. One girl even cried. We went from feeling so beautiful in these gorgeous gowns to feeling insecure and invisible.

Here's my advice to you: Let everyone be beautiful and look their best on your big day. Pick a color scheme or dress styles that flatter the people you've chosen to stand beside you. Ask your bridal party if they would feel good wearing what you're thinking of choosing for them. Don't let anyone talk you into watering down your friends when choosing bridesmaids' dresses or their hairstyle and makeup palette. You shine the brightest when you're being beautiful on the inside. Besides, it doesn't matter if Beyoncé was your bridesmaid—you will still be the one that no one will take their eyes off of. Promise.

THE TRUE TALE OF WHEN SOMETHING WENT RIGHT IN WEDDINGVILLE

by amiira

BEFORE GREG AND I were engaged, I was shopping with a girlfriend at Barneys New York in Beverly Hills. We were looking for something for her to wear to the Emmy parties, so we were in the super fancy dress section of what is my own personal favorite fashion mecca. While we were dress shopping, I saw this truly beautiful, ethereal gown that was almost a gray or muted steel lilac with an organza over-layer and Swarovski crystals sewn inside little pleats, folds, and seams, which sparkled (but not overly so) because they were covered in translucent steel lilac organza. I told my girlfriend, "I would totally get married in that dress. It's gorgeous." It really was. Cut to a few months later when Greg and I got engaged and I started looking at wedding dresses. It was a great season for wedding dresses, and there were many that I looked at that were definite contenders. Unfortunately, the low end of the dresses that I liked was around $5,000; the ones I loved were easily averaging ten grand more.

This was eighteen years ago when I was wedding dress shopping, so I can't even imagine what the prices are now! As we were planning our nonwedding wedding the Barneys warehouse sale was happening. So, along with our dearest fashion-y friends Jackie and Paul, Greg and I made the pilgrimage to the sale. The boys went their way, and Jackie and I went ours. We hit the shoes and bag sections first (as you do) and continued up and down the endless aisles of marked-down treasures. Lo and behold—there was my dress! I couldn't believe my eyes. It was originally $6,500 marked down over and over to $190. No shit!

I grabbed it. I walked out of the Barneys New York warehouse sale with the prize of all prizes—my wedding dress for under $250, tax included. That freed me up to reallocate money on other things—like shoes! It was a moment that I'll never forget and one that Jackie and I often reminisce upon still to this day. Sometimes the universe gives you a most unexpected gift. Fingers crossed that you get lucky in your wedding dress search as well.

• • • •

WHERE DID MY GIRLFRIEND GO?

Greg here. If there's one thing any writer hates, it's knowingly stepping into a cliché or some tired old trope that you've seen in every movie or shitty sitcom since the beginning of time. Tried and true in the wedding world is the classic idea that the feminine partner goes "berserk" during the planning stages of the wedding while the male stands uselessly disinterested to the side just getting in everyone's way. Even in the case of our "nonwedding wedding" it still had to be planned like a wedding. There were guests, a location, food, flowers, cake, invites, table arrangements, a wedding gift registry, and the dress. It's a lot.

Amiira is an original. One of a kind. That doesn't exclude her from being a member of her gender and person who wants to get everything as right as it can possibly be. That's what makes her great. It's also what makes her seem insane sometimes. So I am writing this, from my experience, to other men to prepare them for the wedding planning transformation your bride *might* (emphasis on might) go through and how to deal with it.

First, to succeed, you must be interested (even if you have to fake it—and you will). Most of us are pretty much interested in getting married because we're in love with the girl. So you think, *"Well my work's done. I've chosen the bride."* But you will be asked questions. Many questions. *"What cardstock do you like?" "How long should the stems be?"* While looking at two plates that look exactly the same, you'll be asked, "Do you like periwinkle or sky blue?" Most of them don't have an answer that truly matters in the grand scheme of life.

There is one rule and one rule only: Do not say, "I don't know."

Just pick one. It doesn't matter which one you pick because she already knows her answer. Let me show you.

> HER: Do you think the Greenbergs should sit next to the main table?
>
> HIM: I don't know?
>
> HER: Christ, are you participating in this at all? Do you even care that this is happening? Why do I feel like I'm doing this alone?
>
> HIM: Uh...I just came in to get my phone.

How it should have gone:

> HER: Do you think the Greenbergs should sit next to the main table?
>
> HIM: I think that's a great idea (even if you don't know who the Greenbergs are).
>
> HER: No, I don't think they get along with the Antons. I'm going to put them at table three with the McCarthys.
>
> HIM: That makes sense.
>
> HER: Thank you.

Do you see how easy it is? Just have an answer even if it is the wrong one.

Prepare yourself for this, though: No matter how much you participate, your bride may still be on edge, obsessed, hard to reach, often in tears. It's a cultural phenomenon that even the most punk, feminist woman can still fall into. Deal with it. Draw a bath, give a back rub, show up with pizza, and bite the bullet. She just wants it to be great. Not for her but for everyone. She's trying to create something. Help.

Lastly, while she's trying to make this a spectacular day, it will also feel like it's for everyone but you. And, in many ways, it is. That's how weddings were designed. But keep this in mind: She's doing all this hard work so she can create the best possible scenario where she gives herself to you. She is still that very awesome girl you fell in love with. In the long run it's about you, but in the short-term it's about her, so cut her some slack, give her a wide berth, and, for God's sake, don't say, "I don't know."

• • • •

THE BEST WEDDING
OF ANYONE WE KNOW

Obviously, every wedding is special in its own way, and certainly taste is subjective, so best, second best, or God-awful is all in the eyes of the beholder. The best wedding of anyone we know is actually by far the fanciest wedding that we've ever been to. It was at a gorgeous estate in the Hamptons and absolutely no expense was spared to make it the most beautiful wedding it could possibly be. Hand on our heart; swear to every and all gods, there has never been a spread in any bridal magazine that outdid this wedding. Just when you thought it couldn't get more beautiful or perfect, it did. Our friend, Brooke, the bride, wore a custom Vera Wang gown, as did her entire bridal party, and her hair and makeup were supermodel perfect. And Thomas, the groom, was straight off the most handsome pages of *Esquire*. The degree of attractiveness of the bride and groom—as well as the wedding party and guests—was just off the charts. *(Disclaimer: None of them are actually models by trade—just very attractive humans.)*

Everywhere you looked, there was something special in every detail that conveyed how much thought and effort the bride, groom, mother of the bride, and their wedding planner put into everything. It seemed unfathomable that a wedding could be this exquisite. When Brooke and Thomas exchanged their vows, they both seemed to be levitating with pure joy. They seemed connected and present in the moment and realized that something magical was occurring as they held each other's hands and locked eyes. There was a buzz in the room from the love and energy. The reception was Gatsby-esque and grand under a tent that had transformed the open-air space into a grand ballroom. The food was superb, the décor was stunning, and the band so dynamic that we all danced until the sun almost came up. The reception was an extension of how glorious Brooke and Thomas's love for each other was. It was so amazing that no one wanted it to end.

We left there feeling the promise of new love not only for the newlyweds but also for ourselves. It was a gift. We came to celebrate our friends and left filled with gratitude. That's why it's our Best Wedding of Anyone We Know.

• • • •

THE BEST WEDDING: FIRST RUNNER-UP

The second-best wedding that we've ever attended had the tremendous bonus of the bride and groom, Clara and Brandon, having friends who also happened to be chart-topping music stars. The ceremony was gorgeous, and Clara's dress and styling were completely both wildly unexpected and romantically traditional, as if *Vogue* were doing a Frida Kahlo–inspired wedding editorial. Brandon looked as if he truly couldn't believe that this incredible creature was actually agreeing to be his bride. That's how lucky he felt—you could visibly see it.

That alone would have been enough, but then there was the reception. We don't remember what the food was or what the table settings and centerpieces looked like. We're not even sure who we sat with or where the reception was. What we do remember is that a multi-platinum band with mega-hits performed a few songs acoustically for Clara and Brandon, and the rest of us got to experience it with them. It was so intimate and cool—a real wow moment. Then, after this big-time rock band finished their set, the singer invited the other music stars in the room to come on up to perform for the bride and groom.

(Total sidebar: Out of the three multi-platinum music acts in the room, it was widely known that the one that had already performed was the only one of the acts that is actually any good live— or whose singer could carry a note without a fancy sound mixer sweetening the vocals. So, basically, one band fully challenged the other two bands to step up and perform live without any fancy effects to distract from the actual abilities of the singers specifically. It was awkward and awesome.)

Watching the other singers making excuses as to why they wouldn't sing and trying to downplay the challenge was truly uncomfortable. It felt like a rock rivalry was being born in our midst. The other two rock bands did not perform but rather gave heartfelt toasts to the bride and groom. It was lovely and weird but most of all memorable, which is why it lands in the first runner-up spot on our list.

• • • •

THE BEST WEDDING: HONORABLE MENTION

Sometimes a wedding is just so beautifully simple that the production of it doesn't overshadow the actual event. You don't notice how much time went in to planning every single thing; it just seems effortless. That was the case of our friends Gray and Anthony. They rented a location in the Malibu hills that had a house and a nice chunk of what was seemingly just flat land with a beautiful ocean view. They set up an altar and lined up some chairs adorned with wildflowers and ribbon for the service. For the reception, they kept with the theme of wildflowers and simplicity and brought in a bar and a dance floor. It was like a little stripped-down pop-up restaurant.

The bride, groom, and their attendants got ready in the house, and the caterer used the kitchen. The ceremony began on the cusp of early evening, so the sun was setting in the background and illuminating the couple with an early summer sunlit glow. The only noises you could hear were from nature or the couple and the reverend during the ceremony. It felt like we were in our own private space in time, isolated in nature, with the sun warming our shoulders and bouncing light off of the water, where nothing mattered but the love between Gray and Anthony. It was the kind of wedding where everyone kicks off their shoes and dances barefoot and all worries and cares disappear.

• • • •

THE WORST WEDDING
OF ANYONE WE KNOW

One of our very favorite couples in the world, Maddie and Kent, wanted a very private low-key wedding in paradise with only a handful of their nearest and dearest in attendance. They had just purchased their first home together and were pregnant with their first child. It was a time of really beautiful firsts in their life together. They planned a wedding in Maui at a beautiful hotel where they could be married on a bluff overlooking the ocean by a Hawaiian minister.

Their parents and eight closest friends all booked their flights and hotel rooms for the occasion. Maddie and Kent live in Los Angeles and flew out to Maui a few days early so they could have a quick baby-moon before their honeymoon (because their parents and best friends would all be there in Maui on their honeymoon with them).

Upon arriving in Maui, they watched a baggage carousel empty and discovered that Maggie's bag had been lost. On any given day lost luggage is a bummer. When your lost luggage contains your wedding dress and your wedding rings, it's a bloody nightmare! Now add pregnancy hormones to the mix and you have an inconsolable bride-to-be. Maddie's luggage was never found—like *never*. The bag disappeared like the Bermuda Triangle along with her wedding dress and her diamond eternity wedding band.

Maddie was so distraught and suddenly found herself in the position of needing to find a wedding dress just days before her wedding—at five months pregnant. She went to every possible store the hotel referred her to but couldn't find anything other than a muumuu to fit her expanding figure. Getting married in a muumuu isn't a fucking dream moment to a pregnant woman who was already feeling enormous.

They also had to find wedding bands. To add to the already crumbling nuptials, their parents and closest friends were all flying from Boston and Chicago to Maui for the wedding—in mid-February. But Mother Nature had other plans and dropped a crazy blizzard, closing airports for three full days. None of Maddie and Kent's parents or friends made it to Maui to see the sunset exchange of vows. Their perfect little private wedding was not perfect, but it certainly was private. It was just Maddie, Kent, the minister, and the two hotel employees that acted as witnesses for them.

• • • •

THE WORST WEDDING: FIRST RUNNER-UP

Nico and Sofia met at a winery in Napa and fell in lust with each other over a Pinot and, later, in love over a Zinfandel. They follow wine and food the way others follow a favorite sports franchise or the stock market. Food, wine, and the pairing of food and wine are literally their thing. They are great at it, and if you're ever invited to their home for a dinner party, do yourself a favor and go.

Nico and Sofia decided to have their wedding at the winery they met at and chose a nearby locally renowned "street food" restaurant that specializes in bringing the food sold by street vendors in various different countries to the table for their rehearsal dinner. It should be mentioned that Nico and Sofia are truly adventurous culinary people. Their family and friends? Less so, but game nonetheless.

Nico and Sofia had curated a tremendous dining experience of their favorite, but totally unusual, dishes for the rehearsal dinner. But, as it turned out, the lamb belly bao was undercooked and half of the human beings that were meant to be standing at the front of the wedding ceremony could barely get upright. The stomach cramps, vomiting, and explosions were unrelenting. While Nico and Sofia managed to sweat through the ceremony without coming unhinged, the parents of the groom, two bridesmaids, a groomsman, and three aunts and uncles had to bail out mid-ceremony to seek refuge in the bathrooms. Never have you seen a grayer pallor on a bride and groom. In fact, if you look at the wedding video you can see that Nico and Sofia both look like they're struggling to keep from soiling their wedding clothes. While the other guests enjoyed the reception, Sofia and Nico were laying on the floor of the bathroom with cold compresses on their foreheads holding hands.

• • • •

THE WORST WEDDING: HONORABLE MENTION

Hannah and Connor were a heavy drinking party couple in their first years together, but when they got engaged and decided to start planning for the future, they dialed it back and became homebodies. Many of their friends did not. In the days leading up to the wedding, there were numerous celebratory dinners and gatherings, as well as the bachelor party. A few of their bridesmaids and groomsmen were often either too drunk or hung over when they needed to be there in support of Hannah and Connor or just made a fun event kind of a bummer because they were too messed up. Hannah and Connor were annoyed that their friends weren't toning it down with the partying and often times were embarrassed by their drunken behavior.

At the rehearsal dinner, Hannah found herself taking care of one of her bridesmaids who drank herself into a night of vomiting in the ladies' room. Connor's best man was no better off. He drank himself into such a stupor that he couldn't function on the day of the wedding and was carted off to a rehab facility by his family who genuinely thought he was going to drink himself to death if they didn't intervene. Hannah and Connor's wedding had a wedding party with a bridesmaid who was green with a throbbing hangover and was short not only a best man but also the wedding bands that the best man had on him when he was taken to rehab. The wedding was still beautiful, but there was a real undercurrent of disappointment that all of the planning and best intentions couldn't account for the poor choices their friends made.

WEDDING INSANITY QUOTE #3

"I'm not sure I even like him anymore."

—Jacqueline Florence Dawn Harris,
spoken to her maid of honor
just moments before her ceremony
(BTW, they just celebrated
their 23rd anniversary)

8

the parties
and the panic

S IF THE WEDDING weren't going to be enough, there are other parties to be had to celebrate your love and impending nuptials. These parties tend to be in the last months and weeks before the wedding, and once the parties begin...so does the panic. Panic that the wedding is so close, panic that it's still too far away, panic that you've made the wrong choices, spent the wrong money, and that regret, or guilt, will swallow you whole. With the parties come the pressure that being the center of attention and of time spent usually brings. It's hard to feel both worthy and grateful enough of such spoils (which certainly you are). Truthfully, even though all the parties are meant to be a token of love and admiration, it can all be overwhelming. That overwhelm can breed a new strain of insecurity especially as these celebrations (the bachelorette and bachelor parties especially) are, by design, something that can divide you. Going into the last weeks before you're to be wed feeling any sense of unhealthy division can trigger even the steadiest of humans to become unstable. Don't freak out if you're freaking out.

• • • •

THE BRIDAL SHOWER

The bridal shower is the beginning of the wedding ramp up for the bride. It is meant to be a classy ladylike gathering where you sip mimosas and white wine while making heartfelt toasts about the profound bonds of lady friendship and opening gifts. The task of planning the bridal shower falls on either the mother of the bride, the maid of honor, or the bridesmaids collectively.

The bridal shower is traditionally a brunch held at a nice restaurant or at the home of a bridesmaid or the mother of the bride. There are often games that are brunch appropriate and PG-13 at the raciest. Guests tend to leave with little favors, like a mini vase of flowers, a pretty candle, or the like. See any bridal website or Pinterest for ideas for games, décor, and party favors. Note to the bride: You will be photographed with all the ladies in your life, so plan your shower outfit accordingly. This is also an event you can create a gift registry for. Whether it's bedroom themed or lingerie themed, do your research and register for things you and your groom will get the most enjoyment from.

ANXIETY LEVEL: Low

FEELINGS: Joyful

POTENTIAL FOR DISASTER: Little To None

• • • •

THE BACHELORETTE PARTY

The goal of the bachelorette party is to celebrate the bride's last days as a single woman. It is not to make her throw up or cry. Unfortunately, that happens more often than not. Since the bachelorette is traditionally thrown by the maid of honor, talk with her ahead of time about your limitations and comfort zone. Be clear if what you want is a day at the spa, not a night at the Thunder from Down Under. Every bride deserves to have a sendoff that she'll look back on fondly, not with utter shame or regret. And, while the shower is open to a wide range of family, friends, and acquaintances, the bachelorette party is BFFs only. This is where the ladies let their hair down and let it all hang out. They put on their highest heels, tightest dresses, drink fancy pink cocktails, and dance their asses off. This is where the sexy lingerie is what's in the pretty boxes with bows, and the girls get naughty.

The bachelorette party can be a night on the town wearing penis tiaras or a destination weekend to a beach resort or a decadent trip to Vegas. The only rule is that it's about the bride. While the gang may be sporting bikinis, drinking piña coladas by the pool, or wearing slutty dresses at a nightclub, this is not the time to take on new boyfriends. Boys love to crash a bachelorette party to try to get some action because drunk bridesmaids are often times an easy target. So be sure to look out for your ladies, and don't be afraid to use your outside voice to shut down any Randoms who try to join your party.

ANXIETY LEVEL: Medium
FEELINGS: Vibrating Excitement
POTENTIAL FOR DISASTER: Oh, It's There

BACHELORETTE PARTY
CAUTIONARY TALE

by amiira

ONE OF MY best girlfriends was getting married and wanted a Las Vegas bachelorette party weekend with her bridal party. My friend had great memories of going to Vegas with her friends and the quasi-debauchery that ensued, and she wanted to recreate it with all of us together. However, she was used to doing Las Vegas with her family at the fanciest hotels—staying in suites, dining at celebrity chefs' restaurants, and ordering expensive bottles of champagne. Going to Las Vegas with a bunch of twenty-some-things who were still establishing themselves in their careers and paying off student loans was a budget operation.

We got two adjoining rooms in a mid-level hotel casino that's nowhere near as fancy as the bride-to-be was used to. We lounged by the pool during the day, ordering fruity drinks, and went dancing at night. One of the bridesmaids had a supposedly great bachelor-ette party idea to spice things up: She safety pinned different colored Life Savers candies to a white tank top. Then in big black marker letters she wrote "A Buck for a Suck" on the front. The idea was to make guys pay a dollar to take the Life Saver off of the bride's shirt with their mouths for some raunchy bachelorette party fun.

Now the bride to be is a thoroughbred of a gal, a real class act of a lady. I told her that she didn't have to go along with it. But she's a gamer, and she wanted to do it. She's a good sport, and, besides, she'd had a few drinks. Down at the bar and casino level, the bride, wearing her Buck for a Suck shirt, got approached by every skeevy, gross guy in the place. The billionaires with private jets and hundred dollar haircuts weren't at this hotel, neither were the GQ models. Instead, drunken frat boys and flashy thugs grabbed at her and bit her chest. The fun bachelorette party game spiraled quickly with the gang mentality of all of these guys wanting to get a piece of her, and it suddenly seemed only shades away from a dangerous situation. The bride, having been fondled by strange men, ended up in tears. She was scared and felt violated. It was horrible.

Moral of the story: Know your bride, know your environment, and, when in doubt, lean toward grace not crass, even if crass seems like it would be more fun.

• • • •

THE BACHELOR PARTY

Greg here. Let me be upfront about my feelings on bachelor parties. Bachelor party options depend on where and how you were raised and what matters to you and your bride. To me, the idea of strippers, porn, hookers, and binge drinking sounds depressing. If you saw *The Hangover* and thought, "YES!" you may have missed the point of the entire movie. We've all woken up with a Bengal tiger in our bedroom. That's just a part of being young, and that's a hard thing to want to let go of. And you are going to have to let go of that.

Let's not kid ourselves here. Most people—I'd say a good 85 percent—are about to change their lives completely. Or promise to. They aren't still at a point in their lives where they're going to go out binge drinking with pals five nights in a row. Spontaneous drug- and drink-filled nights and on-a-whim trips to Mexico are probably out. Not because they're a drag or life sucks, but because they've passed that stage of their life already, and it's time for a different kind of adventure with the person whom they've decided is the ultimate. Yes, they will still have grand adventures without their mate. (We dedicate a whole chapter to that.) But as far as nights of degraded debauchery, it's my hope they got enough of that before they made this grand decision to spend the rest of their life with just one girl/guy. Tirade aside, the point is this: if you didn't get enough time being single, it's fair to say that one last night of it isn't going to solve that problem.

For my bachelor party, my best friends and I all went out of for steaks and drinks. It was an evening of hanging out, sharing old stories, talking about music, and having a good time bullshitting. It was just me and my best friends connecting and having some laughs, and it was enough for me. I had a rich single life, so I didn't need to make up for lost time or experiences. Maybe you want to go on a camping weekend, golf, go white water rafting, or go surfing in Mexico for your bachelor party. There are lots of creative ways to celebrate the end of your single life without involving the single-minded objectification of women, the depletion of brain cells, or the fouling of farm animals.

Now this may make me sound like a narrow-minded judgmental prick. Have I objectified women? Yes. Have I been to strip club bachelor parties? Yes. But I didn't dig them. It was all a little bro for me. But some guys go to strip clubs with their ladies, so if it's a part of the fabric of their relationship, then who am I to judge? If your lady is off at *Magic Mike,* then that's how they roll. Good for you. Just make sure it's something you can live with and don't start your marriage off with a secret or a lie.

Leave your single life with the class and elegance you want to enter your marriage.

ANXIETY LEVEL: High
FEELINGS: Nausea/Concern
POTENTIAL FOR DISASTER: Legitimate

• • • •

DEM COLD, COLD FEET

I didn't experience the classic wedding "cold feet." I've felt it about jobs, guitars, and ex-girlfriends, but I did not doubt marrying Amiira. I was sure it was the right decision with every bone in my body, and I never had a thought that threatened to stop me from being where I wanted to be, which was by her side.

But "cold feet" is a very real thing that does happen. It's a flash of fear that asks:

What am I giving up?
Can I live without that?
What am I afraid of?
Can I overcome it?
What's wrong with me?
Can I fix it?
What is wrong with her?
Can it be resolved?

These are all real questions, and it's okay to ask them of yourself. It doesn't make you a bad person for needing to process these fears before you enter into your own marriage. I know because my wife had cold feet. That's right, fellas—it goes both ways. My wife had some very real concerns about me as a person. It was a little embarrassing and hurtful when she brought this stuff up to me, but, if she hadn't, she'd have made a big mistake. She had concerns about my handling of money, about my lack of insurance (there's no Comedian's Union), and about my teeth being a mess. However, her biggest concern was about my ability to mature. She would not marry me until all of these issues were resolved. She wasn't cruel about it, but she wanted to marry a man, not a pile of liability with a removable front tooth.

I'm not going to lie, it burned a little. It felt like I got caught being a child, especially since I'd been working on bettering myself since getting sober. But here's the truth: You will never stop working on yourself, especially in a marriage. Nothing brings out your flaws and your assets like a relationship. But I also handled it "like a boss," as they say. Not all of it in the timeframe she may have wanted but enough for her to know that A) I took her seriously and B) my own life mattered to me.

My wife's cold feet were real, and she addressed them so that they wouldn't bite us in the ass later. If the concern is greater than, "This might fuck up my Wednesday boy's night," talk it out because that conversation after marriage usually goes, "You knew who I was when you married me." Ugly.

WEDDING INSANITY QUOTE #4

"If I had to choose planning a wedding or going on Survivor, *I'd pick* Survivor. *It seems less stressful."*

—David T. (Who sent in an audition for the TV show *Survivor* but was not chosen)

• • • •

TO THE GROOM

I love what my wedding actually became; it truly had that magical quality that even recalling it puts butterflies in my stomach. I was sober for four years, but that day I was as high as I'd been since I'd quit drinking. I remember the amazing rush of saying our vows, like going over a waterfall. I was in. And once our very short ceremony was over, it was a head spinning night of thank yous and kisses. In short, it was like a dream.

But, on the day, Amiira was not interested in my point of view. It's the bride's day. If you want to help, ask her, "Is there anything I can do?" If there isn't, then get the fuck out of the way.

One last thing. Don't get plastered at your wedding. Hopefully this only happens one to three times in your life. Be there for it. Because, if you are not, there is a pretty good chance you won't want to be there for the rest of it.

Good Luck Pal,
Greggers

• • • •

TO THE BRIDE

It can seem like it's taking forever for your actual wedding day to come. Even on the wedding day it takes forever for the clock to roll around to starting time. Time drags on forever until it's suddenly speeding by too fast and you're not ready yet. There's chaos and madness as you pull it all together in those last moments to walk down the aisle. You want to sprint to your groom, but you're shaking too hard and unsure of your equilibrium. Your body is flooded by the rampant firings of crazy new sensations that you want to remember vividly, but they're coming too fast to grasp on to. Your life feels like it is about to really begin.

Be forewarned: You will have an ongoing flurry of questions, thoughts, and fears that pop into your brain up until the moment you are handed your bouquet and sent down the aisle. Don't fight them. You can't win, so just let them flow out of you. Being a bride is like running a mental marathon for a day. There is no way to shut off your overthinking brain—and that's okay. It's all part of the experience that you will laugh about later.

Make yourself a great playlist. Have something delicious brought in for you and your ladies so that you remember to eat and don't get lightheaded at an inopportune time. Make a Build Your Own Champagne drink bar with different juices, champagnes, and berries to loosen everyone up and lift the spirits. Remember to stay hydrated so you don't get drunk before the ceremony. Pace yourself, you beautiful creature. This will be the longest day of your life and the best one. It is your personal zenith and you get to share it with your favorite person on Earth.

Take a moment when you need one. Know that you are completely prepared for today. Everything will fall into place. Enjoy this. Hold this feeling in your heart. Let it calm you and fill you at the same time. This is one of those days that you want to relive over and over again, so don't get caught up in micromanaging details that someone else can handle. Everyone around you wants to help. Let them. Don't let your wedding day memories be you in crisis mode solving logistical problems and massaging the minutiae of every little hiccup. There will be hiccups, but they don't matter, and no one will notice or remember them. Today is the day you are the most smoking hot you've ever been, wearing possibly the most expensive item of clothing you'll ever buy, and the most in love you've ever felt. Run with it!

And have a slice of cake for me!

Amiira xx

9

wedding hangover

*P*OST-WEDDING DAY DEPRESSION (PWDD) is a real thing, and you're certainly not alone in feeling it. It's like the emotional equivalent of an intense sugar rush that's followed by an intense sugar crash. PWDD can leave you feeling depressed and emotionally wasted. However, the old saying is completely true: *This, too, shall pass.* You will feel like your gorgeous, bright self again soon. Post-wedding day depression is not unlike the day after Christmas or the day after your birthday where you feel inexplicably low but amplified really profoundly. It's because the memory of your wedding day is still so fresh and vivid that you can feel it, but the big event is already in the rearview mirror, not ahead of you as something to look forward to anymore.

Take comfort in knowing that there are still so many exciting firsts in your future together that will fill you with such joy and gratitude that they will dwarf the feelings from your wedding day, like getting your first puppy together or spending the first night together in your new house, not to mention finding out you're pregnant or having a baby together—it's incomparable and beyond measure. Those moments are ahead of you. Look forward to the life you will build together, the great adventure you have front row tickets to, and know that PWDD's got nothing on you.

PEOPLE AREN'T ALWAYS HAPPY FOR YOU

THERE WILL BE those who will, with great pride and a small taste of self-satisfied venom, happily tell you (the recently wed) that they don't believe in the binding institution or outdated ritual you have just pledged yourself to. They will say that they don't need the state of California or Allah to bind them in eternal bliss; they are already very happy without all the claptrap of weddings, documents, and the ceremony.

Do not be fooled by these people who refuse to live by the "constraints of modern society." Marriage is not a constraint. It is not a law. It is a choice. Usually one made gleefully and seen as that next "step" in the relationship we call love. And why do we do it? Because we know it is bold and it is meaningful. Therefore, it does not suck—though people, movies, sitcoms, relatives, friends, and, yes, even you sometimes, will think it does.

Marriage is grand and beautiful, uneven and stupid, silly and sad, profound and magical. Most of all, it's yours. And those that mock it will never know it or have the courage to understand it. Congratulations. You're married! Let's move on.

NEWLYWED FORTUNE COOKIE

The grass is greener where you water it, not on the other side.

• • • •

THE HONEYMOON

A wedding can leave a couple frazzled, exhausted, and sometimes even in an out-of-body state. The honeymoon is where you get to recover from the wedding-related stress. So many couples tell us that they didn't even realize how much anxiety they were living with until long after the wedding was over. Your normal state just becomes high anxiety, so you stop noticing it. That's what happens when you spend a lot of money and try to please a lot of people. The honeymoon is the light at the end of an awesome tunnel. You come out of this incredibly emotionally intense experience and get to bask in the glow of romance and relaxation.

We speak from experience when we tell you that the honeymoon may be a once-in-a-lifetime opportunity that you don't want to miss. We kept thinking that we would take a honeymoon later on when we both had more time off. We had both just started new jobs and projects but didn't want to postpone our wedding until we could line it up with newly accrued vacation time. This was a mistake; our honeymoon never happened. Life kept us busy, and our honeymoon trip window never came back around. A baby and a mortgage soon followed, and our vacation window closed, as both are financially exhausting.

Seize the moment and take a honeymoon. When planning your honeymoon, think big—not necessarily expensive—just big. Go somewhere you've never been together as a couple or somewhere you may not ever get to otherwise. Don't skimp on the accommodations, spoil yourselves, and stay in your little newlywed love cocoon where the pressure of the wedding is behind you, and you get to just be and enjoy. Once you return home, it will be back to the reality of thank you cards and going back to work. As Tom Haverford and Donna Meagle say, "Treat Yo' Self!" See Rome or lay on a beach. Rent a private boat like Beyoncé and Jay Z (on a much smaller scale, of course).

Some families divide up the costs of the whole wedding experience between them. The bride's family might pay for the wedding and the groom's family the honeymoon. Or the families may pitch in together to help out with the wedding, but the couple is on their own for the honeymoon. Maybe you are on your own for the whole thing. You still have to find a way to make it happen. That's where you can get creative with your registry items (see page 101).

The Big Three:

A. What is our honeymoon budget?
B. Where should we go?
C. What parts of the honeymoon, or preparation for the honeymoon (like luggage), can we register for?*

Now please, go book your honeymoon. Do it for us and the stupid couples like us that didn't take one when we could have.

---

* The idea of registering for your honeymoon didn't exist when we got married, but now there are registry sites where you can register for every element of a honeymoon, from travel to accommodations, from meals to spa treatments. We just gifted a couple an evening dinner for two at the beachfront restaurant where they were honeymooning and a horseback ride at sunset. Epic!

• • • •

BACK TO REALITY

Crashing back to Earth after what is probably a year plus of living in the hyperreality of wedding planning isn't always a smooth landing. Re-entry into the atmosphere of what will now be your normal existence of your life being about today rather than the wedding. All the things that you've postponed dealing with or doing until after the wedding are now there waiting for you. The life you postponed is upon you now. It's a surreal adjustment to make, living without the omnipresence of your wedding. Not until you are on the other side do you realize how much space in your life it was actually taking up. How your mental focus was always split with part of you always thinking of wedding details and to-do lists. Many newlyweds struggle with finding their footing after the adrenaline rush wears off and their life becomes simple again. There's no shame in feeling sadness that your wedding and honeymoon are now behind you. But it would be a shame not to look at where you stand on the other side as an opportunity for reinvention and design. You are the architect of your lives together with the dominion to now conceive the life you want to have together. The choice is yours together on how you lay out your present and future. It's like planning another big event that doesn't have a shelf life or expiration date. One that won't be over when the calendar changes the date. While you might think that your wedding was the zenith—which it absolutely was for your life up until that day—you have actually just arrived. The wedding was just the two of you going through the really cool turnstile for the ride that will take you to countless other zeniths and adventures you haven't even known to imagine. Back to reality doesn't mean back to boring, it means no more being distracted by cake testings when there's a new life to be lived. Your life has been lived on a timeline, running an obstacle course of wedding planning exercises, to a deadline. (Certainly it was a wonderfully romantic deadline, but a deadline nonetheless.) The excitement doesn't have to be over just because the wedding is.

• • • •

SHAKE IT OFF

When you're struck with those post-wedding blues or blahs the quickest way to crush them is to make a gratitude list. Surely you have much to be grateful for in the face of the malaise you might be feeling. Prepare yourself a cup of tea or pour yourself a glass of wine and get your gratitude on.

Write down three good things that happened to you today.
List three things you saw that were beautiful today.
Name weird things that make you happy.
What five songs always make you want to dance?
What do you wish you could do more of?
Name a happy accident that improved your life.
What do you want to learn this year?
Who do you owe a thank you card to?
What is your luckiest moment?
What can you do to help someone else?

Doesn't that feel good? To have gratitude for all that you do have instead of sadness for something you don't? You have everything you need to be happy in addition to a partner to share it with. Lucky you!

10

newlyweds!

EWLYWED. IT'S A NOUN. It's an adjective. It's a condition of the human experience. Newlywed implies so much more than just being newly wed. Just as every day has its dawn and dusk so does every marriage. The newlywed period is the dawn of your marriage, and dawn rocks (both the grease-cutting dish detergent and the breaking kind of dawn that is filled with vampire and werewolf love triangles). There's this glorious newness to everything you do together, even if you've done it together a million times before.

The newlywed period is one of the greatest periods in your life together as a couple. There's little to no fighting, lots of sex, and your life feels full of possibilities. It's a visceral giddiness combined with a newfound sense of strength and that rush of euphoria that you felt when you first fell in love with your spouse. You no longer stand alone with each other—you stand TOGETHER.

Amiira here. When I think back to when Greg and I were first married, I remember feeling so purely happy, and my life felt so uncomplicated. Happy and uncomplicated are two things that I have tremendous gratitude for because those two bedfellows don't often travel hand in hand in this world once real post-newlywed life takes over. We were absolutely overjoyed to be reunited at the end of our workdays. There was nothing in our little daily world besides us. No major responsibilities, no children, no never-ending to-do list that sucked up our energy and attention, no distractions, no nothing but being newlyweds.

That precious magical "no nothing" time is LIM-I-TED. Just you wait. My days are hijacked by my responsibilities to our kids, their schools, their dance team, our dogs, our house, my work, so on and so forth. I'm underwater all the time and am lucky if Greg and I can complete a conversation at any point in the week, much less luxuriate in each other's company pretty much ever. Not that I'm complaining. I love our life together and all of the time-sucking things that fill it, but if I could drink from the fountain of newlywed invincibility, I'd have that instead of coffee every morning.

Newlywed-dom is like a comet that appears once every fifty years. Get out your telescope, spread out a blanket under the stars, open a bottle of wine, and soak up every moment while you're still in it. The rest of us will be over here seething with a mixture of nostalgia and white-hot jealousy.

NEWLYWED FORTUNE COOKIE

How you want it to end
is how you want it to begin.

• • • •

NEWLYREAL

How different is being married than being engaged? At first it probably seems like it's just a slight difference, maybe just a few degrees to the left of how you were before getting married (especially if you've already been living together). But as time goes by, this difference grows. You grow surer of what you need to exist together in harmony. When you're dating, engaged, or still in the early cohabitation stage of your relationship, you are often the *least* needy and *most* agreeable version of yourself. Little shit doesn't matter because you're in love and getting married. But after you get married the little shit pops up and says, "Remember me? I'm still here!" And, if you don't learn how to manage the little shit, it grows into (seemingly) big shit because it takes on deeper meaning. Suddenly, something that was a nonissue before now leaves one person feeling like they are not being considered and the other persecuted for not being a mind reader.

"That's not us," you think to yourself.

It's everyone. We promise you. Let us give you a couple examples:

We have a friend who loves to play golf on the weekend with his friends. He's done this for as long as we've known him and as long as his wife has known him. She was always totally cool with him spending his Saturdays and sometimes Sundays golfing, especially when she was busy planning their wedding. She was happy to get rid of him for the day. Golfing is something that he loves, and he's always happier after he's golfed. It's his one thing a week that's for him, and she was all for it.

Cut to nine months into their marriage, and she's not all for it or even cool with it any more. Not because she's pulled the old bait-and-switch or tricked him but because she wants to spend her weekends with her husband and not be a golf widow for the next forty years. She thought she was fine with losing her husband for six to eight hours of their Saturday and Sunday, but it doesn't *feel* fine anymore. It feels like he's choosing golf with his friends over time with his wife, even though they had already established this routine.

Golf took on a new meaning for her, and he was completely blindsided by her change of heart. Every time he spent the day golfing with his friends he felt guilty and came home to an unhappy wife. They both felt resentful of the other putting them in a position to feel shitty. It was a sticky subject for a while, and, though they have found a compromise that works for them now, they both spent many tense weekends not getting what they wanted or needed from each other.

This next example can be applied to many habits that one of you might have. We have married friends who have very different jobs. He works in finance and has to be up early while she is a writer and writes more at night and sleeps later in the morning. When she comes to bed, often after he's already asleep, she watches shows on her iPad to get her brain to shut off for the night. She doesn't watch it loudly (in fact, she wears headphones), but the light from the iPad and her reactions to what she's watching usually wake him. Once he's awake, it's hard for him to fall asleep again and often he doesn't. Watching her iPad helps her decompress before going to sleep, and he wants her to have what she needs because he loves her...but he *has* to wake up earlier than she does for work.

He tried to continue being okay with the arrangement that they had in place for the last two years, but tired people can get seriously fucking cranky. He was always overtired and never got the sleep he needed. It felt a lot like she was placing her own need for (unnecessary) entertainment above his need for (vital) sleep. They had numerous bad nights where he ended up sleeping in the guest room, or she never came to bed, and they both felt terrible about it. Ultimately, she had to concede the comfort of watching her iPad in bed and place his needs above her wants, but it still comes up in any argument they have. This iPad versus sleep thing is cemented in their fighting patterns now as a dual resentment.

Like we said, it's the little things that take on a deeper meaning when they don't get flushed out. It's the stuff that you think doesn't matter that becomes a brick in the wall of resentment. We're not saying golfing on the weekends and iPads in bed are the stuff of deal breakers, but things like these can linger in an otherwise healthy relationship. Even a small mountain of these little things adds up to a big thing, and, trust us, you *will* have a small mountain. Little things never stop showing up in life and marriage. Consider yourself lucky if a little mountain is all you have. Most people get their own personal Everest if a marriage lasts long enough. (That sounds super negative, but climbing Mount Everest is not only one of life's greatest destinations but also an unequalled accomplishment...just like marriage.)

• • • •

SO HOW DO YOU NIP
THESE THINGS IN THE BUD?

Here's the key: communication, communication, communication. If that doesn't work, try oral sex. People will agree to anything when that's in play. It's not easy to tell your partner that you don't like things that you pretended to like or thought you could like. It's really hard. You don't want to let them down or have them think less of you, but at the same time, you have to get absolutely honest with yourself about what you can live with and what will make you inexplicably furious.

Find a time when you both are in a good place to bring it up. There's nothing worse than being mid-argument about something else then blindsiding them with an, "...and you know what else? I can't stand it when you blank blank blank" or "...and also? I don't think your friend James is awesome. I think he's a fucking asshole!" Heated times are not the time to approach touchy subjects. That's not fighting fair (something we'll get to later in the book because we've both been found guilty on that charge more than once).

How you approach negotiating the uncomfortable stuff early on will create the patterns for communication in your marriage. It's best to put the effort into doing it well early on. How do you do that? Well, we're firm believers of softening up your person with a little act of kindness then treading lightly into the conversation. Something along the lines of, "I made you a coffee. Do you have a minute? I don't want little things to get between us, and I'm afraid that they will. I wanted to tell you that there is something that I thought I was going to be okay with that is not feeling okay to me anymore. I'm sure you have experienced something like it yourself with me, so I thought we could make a pact with each other that we will try to stay on top of communicating these things and not let them be things that go unsaid or bottle them up inside us." No harm, no foul. Shooting for transparency while you're still early in your marriage will serve you as a couple and as individuals forever.

• • • •

TRANSCRIPT FROM
AMIIRA AND GREG'S REAL LIFE

We are very different people. Greg is a sensitive, creative person, but he is also very forgetful because his mind is filled with a constant flow of ideas and fantasies. Amiira is much less sensitive, and she likes things buttoned up pretty tightly, and she nearly never forgets anything. It's not a match made in heaven on that specific level; in fact, it's at times a nightmare for the both of us. We had to find a way to accommodate this discrepancy that would come up in our daily lives. In the early days of our marriage, our little daily issues sounded like this...

AMIIRA: Why is the orange juice in the pantry?

GREG: I don't know.

AMIIRA: I didn't have orange juice today.

GREG: I didn't either. I had it yesterday.

AMIIRA: So, the perishable orange juice has been in the pantry for two days?

GREG: I don't even remember putting it there.

AMIIRA: Your car keys are there, too.

GREG: I ruined the orange juice and lost my keys. At the end of the day no one got hurt, right?

AMIIRA: Not really.

GREG: You treat me like I'm a child.

AMIIRA: Well a grownup knows how to put away orange juice.

[Fight ensues. This is clearly about a bigger issue.]

On it would go with the two of us fighting over something that was completely insignificant but clearly triggered bigger things within us. Greg felt caught doing something stupid, and Amiira was caught being a bitch because the orange juice in the wrong place activated a bigger fear of things feeling out of control and not buttoned up like she likes them. It wasn't the actual orange juice that was the issue; it was the way Amiira approached the conversation. Amiira often speaks too quickly and doesn't think about the best approach to communicating with Greg. It took us quite some time to figure it out so that we both felt heard and could address just one issue without making it an avalanche of verbal debris.

Here's how the conversation would go if approached in a thoughtful manner considering both party's feelings and own weird personal trigger points.

AMIIRA: Who's the super creative funny guy who left the orange juice in the pantry?

GREG: Was it me?

AMIIRA: I hope so or else the ghost of Mitch Hedberg is haunting our house.

GREG: I'll try to remember to put the juice back in the fridge.

AMIIRA: Thanks.

GREG: Have you seen my keys?

AMIIRA: Nope.

See how Greg's feelings don't get hurt, and Amiira *still* gets to make him search for his keys? It's the little things that will make your relationship thrive. By the way, marriage is just helping your person find or *not* find their keys until one of you dies or you get divorced. You'd be surprised how many divorces are a by-product of being driven crazy by the continually lost keys loop.

• • • •

CELEBRATION AND CEREMONY

When you're still brand new, everything about you, your spouse, and your love involves a fair amount of ceremony and pageantry. Things like birthdays, Valentine's Day, anniversaries of all kinds all get a lot of attention, planning, and play. There is a level of spoiling each other that is absolutely lovely. Nothing seems more important than getting these big moments right. After you get married and your lives are joined, you settle into your new life. The expectation of the level of ceremony often evolves—usually things go from being a big deal to being less of a big deal, if not a small deal. It's not the first birthday you're spending together, so you may not go as full out. Maybe you no longer celebrate the anniversary of your first date or half anniversary of the day you became engaged, especially now that you have a wedding anniversary to celebrate.

Not celebrating everything as big and boldly as you once did doesn't mean that there's any less love there between you, but sometimes it can feel like that. Actually, there's an argument to be made that it might mean that there's more love because your spouse is no longer trying to impress you with pageantry; instead, they're being authentic. Once you're married, it's no longer the endless audition of your best underwear. You will see your person every day for the rest of your life, and some days you just want to wear comfortable panties, not decorative ones that have to be hand laundered in lukewarm mineral water and laid flat to dry.

Remember, communication is key in marriage. So, if you want to continue with the kind of ceremony and pageantry that you had during your courtship and engagement that's totally cool. However, let your spouse know that's how you feel. If you are someone who loves Valentine's Day, you have to let your person know that the undying romantic in you will always need that day to be a big deal. Tell them that you still want to celebrate the anniversary of your first date, as well as your wedding anniversary—you can't expect them to be mind readers.

You are morphing during the newlywed years and finding what will become your new normal. Truth be told, once you have kids you may not have as much time for the ceremony and celebration, and it falls away naturally. But what and how you celebrate your special occasions only have to work for you and not anyone else. There is greatness and wonder coming your way and no shortage of times to celebrate.

• • • •

NEWLYWED CHECKLIST

As you ease your way into married life, here is a simple checklist for you to refer back to that will help remind you of all of the good things in your marriage.

1. Have gratitude for your spouse, gratitude for your love, gratitude for your life together. You've just won the life lottery.
2. Have respect for your differences, respect for their traditions, respect for their feelings, respect for their opinion, respect for their family and friends.
3. Have empathy in difficult and trying times. Hurting someone doesn't help anyone.
4. Let go of things that don't matter. Listen instead of talk. Not everything needs a conversation or an acknowledgment. We're all human.

5. Adapt. Be willing to evolve both individually and together. Holding on too tight to anything will only result in suffocation. We don't need to stay so set in our ways.

6. Be here now. Enjoy what you have, and don't try to rush into the future when the present is so beautiful.

7. Hold hands often.

8. Count your lucky stars.

9. Say, "I love you."

10. Be kind instead of right.

11

marrying your lives

A N IMPORTANT PART OF being married is knowing when to yield and when to merge. Marriage is like playing bumper cars forever. You can bump into each other for fun or sport, but you can also really bump into each other in that not-so-passive-aggressive "I am really hating your guts right now" way, as well. You are combining your friends and your families, your furniture, your pets, and your lives in general. Much in this process is more loaded than it seems because you are uniting the things that you hold most dearly.

Yes, it could be said that this is the opportunity to get rid of his furniture, but that would be shallow (*do it*) to even discuss (*no, seriously, do it*). You each come with your own stuff in your bumper car, and your stuff will be important to you and theirs will be important to them. As you bump along side by side in your cars, you both will lose some stuff, break some stuff, and hold on tightly to stuff. But remember that, when it comes down to it, stuff is just stuff. It holds very little value when it stands next to the person you love.

Mark our words: Your lives together will be an ongoing purging of stuff, so don't die by the sword of anything that can be bought because it can always be bought again. The really hard stuff in the yielding and merging of your lives is navigating your families' traditions and honoring yourselves, as well as the importance of any historical ties (meaning what in you or your spouse's own history holds great importance, either emotionally, spiritually, or traditionally).

The first couple years of marriage are when you try out a bunch of different things to see how they feel as a couple. What routines do you establish for yourselves in your daily life? How are vacations and holidays decided upon? What is the timeline for buying a home or starting a family? Is there still room in your life for all the things you did before you were married? When do you yield to your spouse's way of thinking or doing? When do they yield to yours? And when do you merge?

This might all seem effortless to you at first. You seem to merge everything seamlessly with barely a conversation needed. That seems right, it feels right, and for the most part is right—except for the barely a conversation needed part. No conversation will bite you in the ass later. A conversation, even if it seems like it's silly and unnecessary, is not just a conversation. It's a sign of respect.

• • • •

HAVE A CONVERSATION

What are the conversations that you should have when you're newlyweds, other than whether to have dinner or sex first?

(BTW, the answer is dinner first, *House of Cards* while you digest dinner, sex, then after-sex snack.)

Conversations should run the gamut from how to divide up household responsibilities (cooking, cleaning, laundry, grocery shopping, paying bills, home maintenance, errands, chores) to discussing your savings plan, when to start a family, and finances in general. You are creating a shorthand that will have long-term effects on the unspoken ebb and flow of how things get done and who does what.

But beware: Feathers can get ruffled when there's a huge imbalance in the yield-to-merge ratio. Now it's entirely possible that each of you may be used to doing things the way you like doing them and just want the other to yield to your (clearly better) way of doing things. That's how it was with us. Amiira is a planner and a doer. She's all about the most linear and economical way to do everything very well. She likes to be informed and prepared, and because of that, she sees the world through that lens and plows forward in a take-no-prisoners manner. Greg, on the other hand, is a circuitous wanderer who plays things by ear and gets things done very differently, on a much slower and more scattered scale. But he gets things done; he's not lazy by any means. He just does things his own way in his own time. When we met, his apartment was a museum of male cleanliness and cool, so why did it seem like he wasn't that way when we were together? It's only because he does things in a roundabout way, and, as a result, he acquiesced to Amiira's way of doing things most of the time, mostly because Amiira is impatient. Amiira would plow forward and do things herself so she could check things off her list while Greg stepped aside. Greg was happy to yield and Amiira was happy to not change. *(Amiira note: Yes, I am difficult to live with.)*

Greg did more yielding than we did merging, and that seemingly worked for us for many years. But Amiira didn't realize that doing things her way most of the time made Greg feel bad. Her need to power through or do as she had done previously created an imbalance and made Greg feel like he had little say in our lives. That, my friends, is not a sexy place for your partner to be.

Moral of the story: Even if your partner is happy to acquiesce, don't always let them because it's not good for either of you. Find a balance where you both feel like you are equally yielding and equally contributing to the harmony of the life you establish together.

When it comes to merging families and friends, remember that blood runs deep and friends run loyal. Your spouse's best friend might be beyond challenging for you, and your spouse may totally acknowledge that, but that doesn't mean that they'll be okay with seeing less of their friend once you're married. Before you existed, that friend might have taken a figurative bullet for your spouse and have forged a bond so deep that your spouse cannot back away from it easily.

Same goes for family. Even the most batshit crazy in-law will inspire an allegiance that is puzzling. You will both be forced to deal with unsavory people and events from your person's previous single life. Merge and yield with great awareness, empathy, and care during these newlywed years, and you will reap the rewards for the rest of your life together.

NEWLYWED FORTUNE COOKIE

Give your partner the best of you, not just the rest of you. No one's really crazy about left overs.

• • • •

HOLIDAZE:
GREG'S STORY

For a very long time, I was one of those people they make horrible Christmas movies about. A guy so rigid, uptight, and opinionated on how the holiday is supposed to take place that it's virtually impossible to please him. Ultimately, he ends up ruining the day for himself and everyone around him by not letting go of his holiday ideals. I'm like an inverse Scrooge.

I grew up in a household that had wonderful Christmas traditions. Those traditions had nothing to do with Jesus and everything to do with eating, drinking, and waiting for the arrival of the fat man. My mother took it very seriously, as did my father. When it came time to have my own family, I wanted to pass those traditions or rituals on. But I married a woman who didn't give two fucks about Christmas. It was a nonevent for her. It wasn't until Amiira and I married that I spent my first Christmas away from home, and I was in my mid-thirties. It was weird.

Whatever your traditions, whatever fondness you had for any of your childhood holidays, know that those are now over, or have mutated. I wish I had known this at the beginning. I wish someone had sat me down and said, "What you had is gone. It's time to create something new. Stop pouting and take off the Santa suit." It would have made life a lot easier for everyone.

Having an attachment or even a nostalgia for your past holidays and traditions is not uncommon, and there is nothing wrong with pining for that. Some people will be thrilled to have a partner who is so dedicated to their family or their traditions, but ultimately there must be some give and take.

• • • •

HOLIDAZE:
AMIIRA'S STORY

Greg and I first started dating around the holidays. Christmas time was especially magical that year because two of my best girlfriends and I were asked to house-sit at a friend's ranch in Malibu. This little ranch had three miniature horses and some other animals that needed looking after. It was the best Christmas a girl in her late twenties could imagine—not kidding! We took our dogs, cooked a ton, drank wine, and watched movies. We tried to remember to call our families occasionally. We did not get a Christmas tree. We did not put up stockings. We did not do anything that would indicate Christmas. We were more concerned with making sure we had the fixings for mango habanero margaritas and enough DVDs to binge-watch in the pre-Netflix days.

Greg came to visit me at the ranch for a day, and it was a blast. It was the first time we slept in a bed together, and we just held hands and cuddled. It was very sweet, and it made the trip that much better.

Christmas held value to me as a young girl for obvious childhood wonder reasons, but as I became a working gal, the value became more about paid time off from work. When I was single, Christmas break was about where I was going to travel and what I was going to do with whomever I was involved with more than sticking to any set holiday rituals. I've spent Christmases at budget spas in Mexico, ski trips with boyfriends (even though I barely ski), visiting my family, hanging around New York with friends, hanging around L.A. with friends, etc. I liked to mix it up during holiday time. I adore my family, but I would pick a fancy vacation over spending time with anyone at Christmas any day of the week. I'd be delighted to combine the two in the best-case scenario.

When I married Greg, I didn't realize that I had married into his very rigid idea of how the Christmas holiday needed to be celebrated. When we went to his parents' home for Christmas, I saw the rituals in their top form. But if we weren't going to be at Greg's parents' for Christmas—and often that was the case—he wanted to recreate all the rituals. I played along because it was clearly important to him, and he was important to me.

But after the first few Christmases celebrated Greg's way, I began to resent how much preparation and time it took from me. There had to be a Christmas Eve dinner party that resembled Thanksgiving-level feast proportions (that I had to shop for, prep, and cook, as well as set the table and clean the dishes). Then after dinner, Greg would slip out and change into a Santa suit and bring everyone new pajamas (that I had to shop for and wrap). Then there was the Christmas morning gift exchange and brunch (which I had to shop for, prep, wrap, assemble, and cook). It was all left to me to execute while Greg got to just enjoy Christmas like he did at his parents' house as the recipient not a participant.

By our third year of marriage, I went from not giving a crap about Christmas to hating Christmas. He put so much weight on it being exactly perfect that it was crushing for me. The thing was that, while I was playing the role of parent, he was still playing the role of the kid at Christmas because that's how it had been for him until he married me. Even as a grown man his parents would spoil him at Christmas, which was very sweet but also mind-blowing for me.

For my family, Christmas had gotten smaller once my brother and I left the house. Pulling off Greg's magical Christmas each year stressed me out, killed my Christmas spirit. I was never happy, which made him unhappy that I was a scrooge, and we'd fight. It took *ten years* for us to get past this because he wouldn't let go of recreating his family's Christmas rituals, and I resented the position I was being put in at every holiday.

It wasn't lost on me that Greg's grandmother's and his mom's passing within the first years of our marriage and his father's subsequent absorption into his new girlfriend's family might be the reason he was holding on to the past so tightly. I should have just sat him down and said, "I love your mom, but let's create our own thing because I don't want to always be put in the position of executing your family's Christmas."

Eventually, we did get past this issue. Greg saw the stress and expectations he was putting on me and our daughters and even on himself. He finally let go of the ghost of Christmas past and has made the holiday about the girls. He listens to music and decorates the Christmas tree with our oldest daughter, who shares his Christmas spirit. And he's open to compromise now when it comes to the holidays. It took time, but he finally yielded, and together we've found our groove with Christmas. And we mix it up, sometimes staying home, sometimes visiting family or friends. The only must-have ritual is to watch the movie *Elf* at some point over the break and make red velvet pancakes on Christmas morning.

Moral of the story: It's never too late to amend the things you didn't get right.

• • • •

SET YOURSELVES UP TO WIN

Here is the key to longevity and health in your marriage: Set yourself up to win. That means thinking ahead and installing some safeguards to protect yourselves from becoming a cliché. For example, if you don't want to be married to a sixty-year-old child, then don't baby your spouse when you're newlyweds. If you don't want to spend your later years with a partner that won't talk about things, break that habit now.

We often hear couples bitching about their spouses' shortcomings, peccadillos, and inabilities to do what one of them considers simple shit. It's all small stuff in the scheme of things, but it represents bigger stuff, and it takes on a different weight when attached to the bigger stuff. You know what we're talking about—you see it in television and movies all the time. One partner remarks pointedly to a group, often in front of their spouse, *"He'd forget his own head if I didn't hand it to him."* Or, *"She couldn't balance a checkbook if her life depended on it."* Seems like harmless stuff, but it's not. They have the underlying subtext of, *"He's an idiot."* Or, *"She can't take care of herself."* These passive-aggressive musings just fan little nagging sparks until they become an actual fire.

It didn't start off like that. It used to be cute when your spouse needed you or was helpless in their own little tiny isolated way that only you ever see. However, when you do everything for your spouse, you end up training them to become helpless and dependent like a child. You know what's not sexy? Children. Ever. Caretaking can feel so good in your newlywed years, but someday it will turn a corner and stop feeling like an act of love and start feeling like an act of obligation. When the newlywed glow wears off—and it will wear off—the simple patterns you set up together, both as willing participants, start to build into bitterness and a loss of respect.

The give a man a fish and he'll eat for a day, but teach a man to fish and he'll eat his whole life adage can absolutely be applied to your marriage. One of you can't always be the fisherman, even if it feels good to be the fisherman (except for the putting worms on hooks and having to gut fish and all that gross bullshit that fishermen have to deal with).

Another tip? Don't always divide up the to-do list the same way. When you have a newborn and haven't slept more than two hours at a time at night for months and there's no food in the refrigerator and the laundry pile is mountainous because you're the only one who grocery shops or does laundry, you will lose your fucking mind. Set the pattern early. Be capable partners who can not only support each other but do so without being asked or told to. It's your job to teach your person how to fish (and their job to teach you). Go ahead and treat yourself to a pair of His and Hers, His and His, or Hers and Hers fishing rods early in the marriage, and enjoy the all-you-can-eat seafood buffet you'll be dining on for eternity.

• • • •

INDEPENDENCE AND TOGETHERNESS

Greg here. Have you read Shel Silverstein's *The Missing Piece Meets the Big O*? The missing piece goes looking for a piece to complete it so it can be happy, until the piece meets the Big O. The piece learns from the Big O that the best relationships are where you complete yourself and roll along together with another rather than expecting them to complete you. There, now you can say you read it.

Independence is sexy. At least to healthy people it is. It was no doubt one of the things that attracted you to your partner. Standing on your own two feet in your new marriage is a good thing. It doesn't mean being alone—that's isolation. There's a difference between independence and isolation. You can be an independent person and work with someone. You can be an independent thinker and still love someone. It is possible and necessary to be independent in the context of your marriage. If you isolate in your relationship, you are not independent. You are alone.

As newlyweds trying to learn how to be together, it's important to know about a few things. Picking up after someone, taking better care of someone than they take of themselves, not letting someone figure out how to do something in their own way, keeping someone from falling—it all *feels like helping*. It feels like showing love, but, in fact, you are isolating that person and yourself. You are putting the both of you in two camps: those who do everything and those who do nothing. Remember, newlyweds: All the seeds of independence get sown early.

Letting someone take care of you is just as isolating. And you are just as guilty for not saying, "Stop, I got this." Sometimes we con ourselves into thinking that getting help from the other person is also helping them. It's not. It's of paramount importance that you protect your independence, for if you don't it will come back to bite you both in the arse.

I'm an odd duck. I used to do things in a strange pecking order for years. But it didn't suit Amiira, who's type A, so I let her do things for me the more expedient way. Or, rather, I decided I didn't know how to do things I'd already done for years—like dishes and laundry—because she had a way she liked them done.

Do you see what I'm saying? It robbed me of my independence. Finally, the dam breaks, and you, a once fairly together guy who's stopped acting like one, is told he has all the instincts of a teenager. What happened to me?

Eventually, I spoke up: *"Look, I do things in a weird way, but the dishes will make it into the dishwasher and table will get wiped down. I will do it."* Type A Amiira has a hard time with the idea of letting things sit. Dishes in the sink sound like yelling to her, and she can't work if there's clutter because her head isn't clear. She decided the way I do things isn't going to work for her, even if I said I hear her and can do it. It's an impasse that has to be managed. Her not being able to tolerate me doing things my way cripples us. By letting her do everything and me not even trying, I cripple us. So, if your partner says they'll try, let them. Give them independence from your way of doing it. They may not be great right away, but, if they are the good person you thought you married, they'll get there.

Loving everything about your partner—and vice versa—is not important. And over the long haul you see that doesn't matter. What does matter is that you hold on to who you are and what you love because that is the person you married.

You learn to tolerate the little things—their feet dragging or getting into bed too loudly. But things that define who you are, however, cannot easily be given up. For anyone. The second you begin to shortchange you on the person you want to be to make someone else comfortable is the day you start to give up your hard-won independence. Conversely, the day you suddenly decide you can't stand your person's music, shirt—whatever—and try to shape or manage the life of your most favorite person in the world, you have to ask yourself, "Why am I taking this from them? When did this thing make me so mad or strike me the wrong way?"

Your partner and you are still growing up and always will throughout the course of your marriage. That haircut your person got, or that pair of boots they wear, or that video game they love so much may just be a phase in their constant evolution, and while it may never be your taste, why don't you look at the bigger picture and see if you can understand it. Or just love them for being different than you. Who knows? You may change your mind, or they may change theirs. The great news is that you don't have to, and you can still be together rolling along side by side like the Big O and the missing piece.

12

touchy
subjects

ERE'S THE MILLION-DOLLAR QUESTION. How do you handle the touchy subjects? The super weirdness that comes in varying forms and degrees. We get asked all kinds of questions that require a heavy-duty amount of thought and consideration. For example, when is it okay to take off your wedding ring? Go to a strip club? Be a single friend's wingman or woman? Not come home at night? Make out with another person? Touch another person in their bathing suit area? Get naked for someone other than your spouse? For the majority of couples none of this is a real nagging issue. For others it's not so cut and dry, and just reading those ideas puts even us on edge.

Perhaps your spouse is an OBGYN and therefore is always sticking their hands in another person's bathing suit area. Maybe your spouse is a nude figure model for a prestigious art school or an underwear model. We've all seen what underwear models' lives look like. Tell us there's not some jealous mate fuming back home while their *Sports Illustrated* swimsuit issue model is off in the Maldives frolicking in the surf with nary a triangle of fabric covering their nether regions while some worldly photographer with a fetching accent coaches them to look more fuckable. That's gotta be great for the spouse back home.

But for some couples, this is a real issue, and it's up to the couple to communicate a way to make days of supremely surreal discomfort as bearable as possible. To nip any possible grudge in the bud. Now, we can't anticipate what strange situations your life has in store for your marriage, but you most likely can. It's up to you to look into your own crystal balls or iCalendars and use your foresight to see if there's anything that will come up so that you can protect yourselves and prepare yourselves for the weirdness.

To accommodate for these weird situations, you and your mate must have three things locked up tight.

1. You must establish such a supreme level of trust that you can be honest and vulnerable with each other.
2. You must share the goal of preserving your new marriage above all else.
3. You must talk out an agreement of what will feel okay, what will absolutely not feel okay, what you think you and your spouse can realistically handle, and what will be a ticking time bomb.

Marriage is not meant to be the *Hurt Locker*, even if you have to suit up a couple of times in your marriage in your full bomb squad gear.

NEWLYWED FORTUNE COOKIE

Don't lie.

Don't cheat.

Don't make promises you can't keep.

• • • •

SLIPPERY SOCIAL MEDIA

Remember when we were talking about setting yourself up to win as a couple in these first couple years of marriage? A gigantic MUST MUST MUST is setting clear ground rules and boundaries for your relationship. Boundaries need to be agreed upon because when two people interpret the same thing differently, as they *often* do, it can lead to a whole world of hurt. Especially in the age of social media and technology, things can get misread, tones can be assumed, and we can innocently get ourselves into sticky situations. You know each other and love each other more than anyone else on Earth, but even your remarkable connection won't save you from stepping on some relationship landmines. Some landmines are in the form of behaviors that surprise you. Some are unmet expectations. Even in your bliss, you will find yourself let down or even crushed by your spouse over things that you just thought would be different or that you feel differently about now that you're married.

For instance, you have committed to forsake all others when you got married, and, yet, with smartphones and social media, an innocent "like" on someone's post can turn into flirtation. Operating behind the veil of social media can create sticky situations, and both of you can be susceptible to it. There have been many times that people we know and love have been caught in this landmine.

One person posts a selfie of them looking cute, and a bunch of their social media "friends" like it, thumbs up it, and comment. Then the spouse of the one who posted sees the comments and clicks on the stranger who commented something sexy or provocative, and down the rabbit hole they go. It's a giant can of worms that can start a horrible cycle of mistrust and suspicion.

The same thing can happen in the workplace. A work flirt can simply be a very light, easygoing friendship with its own little spark and be completely harmless. But it is not harmless to your spouse. Be proactive about this kind of stuff and set some boundaries; otherwise, the digital age of friendships and light flirting becomes quicksand. While you can't control how other people behave, you can be transparent about who your digital and professional friends are and which, if any, make your spouse feel uneasy.

In our case, when we've had digital "friends" toe or cross our set boundaries, we've unfriended or blocked those who seem to either have an agenda that doesn't support our marriage or just causes too many bad feelings. We've pulled away from other acquaintances that seem to be loaded with uncertain motives. Nothing is more important than your relationship or your marriage, so don't let toxic things or people exist in your world, if you can help it.

Finally, put your spouse first. Have their back. Don't pick your friends, relatives, or work over them when at all possible. Yes, there will be times when you are tested and in a seemingly impossible situation where you just cannot put your person first. But if your person has no doubts about where they stand in your priorities, you will be able to navigate the impossibilities hand in hand.

• • • •

BECOME THE MCPLANNERSONS

Amiira here. So, you're newlyweds. This is the time to live it up, do what you want to do, and spend time with each other—you won't have this time again. While you're living it up, make some financial plans for the future. We've seen the future, and it's fucking expensive. Our plans were pretty straightforward when we were newlyweds: buy a house, have a baby, totally wing it as to how to pay for the house and baby. I left my job before we got married when we began writing together. We decided to bet on ourselves instead of being a slave to The Man. Honestly, I should have been a slave to The Man for a few years longer, racked up some more of that sweet, sweet steady income, and milked The Man for all I could in maternity benefits. My bad.

Being two adults who work in the creative arts is not the most predictable, consistent, or dependable living to be made, so we went through some pretty stressful times of poor planning and money management. We drained our savings accounts to put the down payment on our first house. By the time we moved in, we had to borrow our first mortgage payment from our parents. Neither of us understood closing costs or how much money you have to shell out for inspections, appraisals, and things we had never heard of when entering into the glorious nightmare of home ownership. We took a lot of leaps of faith in our newlywed years and blew it a few times.

If your circumstances allow it, take it from us Oldyweds and be the McPlannersons. Financial stress is a romance killer and one of the biggest problems for all couples, so take the opportunity to be smart about your financial future. *(Side note: If you're on your second marriage, already have kids, or a life that barely slowed for your wedding, we feel you, and we applaud you because you already know the struggle, and the struggle is real.)*

What should the McPlannersons plan for? It's a lot of super exciting stuff, like picking good insurance plans: health insurance, life insurance, homeowners/renters insurance, car insurance. Are you getting turned on yet? Just wait until we start planning for your financial future. Want me to talk dirty to you? Ohhh—consolidating debt, joining bank accounts, agreeing on a budget, figuring out a savings strategy, setting up a timeline for your life goals. It's not stuff that is exciting to talk about in the tradition-building sense, but it's stuff that matters greatly in the big picture of your future. If you plan for it, you'll be prepared for it; if you don't plan for it, you'll be swallowed by it. You gorgeous newlyweds get to be the architects of your own love story, and that love story is only made sexier when you couple spontaneous wonder with responsible actions. Planning is sexy because taking care of each other is super sexy, and making sure your future is getting a fair amount of forethought is next-level sexy.

When Greg and I got married, we knew we wanted to start a family and hopefully buy a house. We wanted to move to somewhere that was a bit more family-oriented and had fewer porn theaters. As I was over thirty, my biological clock made our timeline feel pretty compressed. This is not a unique situation and certainly there are different factors besides a biological clock that can affect your timeline. That's why sexy planning is so important, so that you can go to sleep at night feeling sorted instead of lying awake with anxiety every other night.

Let's talk plans and timelines. They should be firm, but not inflexible. What do you see for yourselves in the next couple years? What about five years? Ten years? Is there an order to be established? When you lay out a timeline for the next five years, what is on it? Mine would have read like this:

Year One:

Join finances

Consolidate debt and appropriate monthly funds to pay ASAP

Research life insurance plans

Travel somewhere

Buy a car

Set new budget

Year Two:

Get pregnant

Buy a house

Work less while pregnant

Buy a baby seat for the car

Set new budget

Year Three:

Have a baby

Stay home with the baby

Trade the car in for van

Set new budget

Are you seeing a pattern here? With every big thing that comes your way, your financial needs and status will change. As you have more, you will also have less.

• • • •

MARRYING YOUR MONEY

Once you're newlyweds, it's time to marry your lives. Even if you've lived together for a while, chances are you haven't fully combined your lives. We're talking about combining your mobile phone plans, auto insurance policies, and health insurance plans and converting them to family plans. Is there a surname change to be made? How are you filing your taxes? Joint, individual, or tax evasion all the way? It means deciding if you're going to completely combine your financial assets or keep separate but open one joint account for checking and one for savings so that you can pay for your life together and save for your life together.

Tip: If there is a great imbalance in the financial earnings or savings between the two of you, figure out what feels fair. For example, maybe you each put 50 percent of your paycheck into the joint checking, 20 percent into the joint savings, and keep 30 percent in your personal accounts. If you each contribute the same percentage of your paychecks, you each take the same financial hit to pay for your lives.

▶ The 50 percent in the joint checking would cover your fixed costs (rent/mortgage/insurance/utilities/credit card payments).
▶ The 20 percent in the joint savings would go towards your financial goals (down payment for a home/trip to Fiji/college fund for kids).
▶ The 30 percent in your personal account is for your own flexible spending (clothes/entertainment/gifts).

As a newlywed, you really get a clear picture of how your spouse spends money, and it can be alarming. When we were first married, we had some savings and steady paychecks and were not thrifty at all. We spent it because we had it and because we had no real big financial responsibilities. Then we bought a house, had a baby, and spent all our savings. It wasn't pretty. We found ourselves behind the eight ball because we didn't budget first and then didn't stick to the budget later. We're sure we're probably the only ones this has ever happened to.

• • • •

CURVEBALLS

Even with the best intentions and best laid plans, life will run you off course many times during your marriage. Certainly during your newlywed years. Sometimes curveballs are glorious surprises, like one of you got an incredible job offer that quadruples your salary. YAY! But you have to move across the country away from all your friends and family where the weather is horrid most of the time, and you'll never really see each other, as the new super awesome job is completely time consuming. BOO!

How does this new curveball fit into your plan? Is this something worth altering your plan for? What could a new plan be? Do you roll the dice on a big paycheck and hope it doesn't leave one or both of you feeling unhappy?

Sometimes the curveball is a shit storm, like when one of your parents is suddenly ill, and you have to become their caretaker. It requires more time than you have, compromises your ability to do your own job, or meet your end of the responsibilities at home. Suddenly, the timeline on your life plan is forced to adjust, and the things you once wanted will have to go on the back burner while you deal with the bad curveball that life threw your way.

We've had tons of curveballs thrown our way, as has every married couple we know. Even when a clear and uncomplicated new path seems to lay itself at your feet, another curveball can turn the clear to cloudy and the uncomplicated to complex. Life is like that, and so are people. We humans evolve, constantly shifting with the tides. We change our minds for any number of reasons, sometimes because a curveball came our way, other times because we threw the curveball ourselves. While curveball change can be exciting, it can also be uncomfortable. Who better to face a curveball with than your best friend, soul mate, newly-wed partner in crime? There is no one we'd rather come home to share the news that we've been fired or won the lottery with than each other. (Obviously we'd prefer the lottery one, but we don't always get to choose.) Our advice to you is hold on tightly to your spouse but loosely to your plans.

13

fighting married

Oh, the Things You Will Fight About...

We're perfect together, we fit like a glove
We're all bundled up and we're bursting with love.
There's nothing to fight about, nothing to see
There's nothing but love between you and me.
We think like each other, we both share a brain
We only give pleasure and never have pain.
We only give high fives and never complain
We're perfect together and totally sane.
We agree about everything, no matter how small,
What to eat, what to watch, we've never hit a wall.
The big things are easy, like money and kids,
No resentments growing, there's nothing we've hid.
'Til we did.
You might think you've said it, you thought that they knew
They assure you they didn't, and off you can screw.
I've always been like this you yell from the yard.
It's not what I signed up for, why is this so hard?

You're being an asshole, you're being a shrew
It's no wonder why my friends all hate you.
Seething with anger, balled up like a fist
Suddenly reconsidering a forbidden tryst.
I don't even like you, let alone love
How I married you, I can't even conceive of.
In the morning it's over, the darkness turned light
I feel like a fool, my behavior a blight.
It wasn't right.
I'm sorry I shouted and called you those names
I didn't really mean it, I'm so filled with shame.
It won't happen again, my temper won't flare
Our marriage won't be the stuff of nightmares.
Can we reset the clock? On that fight press delete?
Have a do-over, start a blank sheet?
You are my one and only, the love of my life
The one I will follow, into the afterlife.
No more trivial disputes, no more fights that are stupid
Imagine the look on the face of poor Cupid.
We're still perfect together, you're still my best friend.
My love for you will always transcend.
'Til the end.

• • • •

FIRST FIGHT CLUB

Greg here. I can't tell you what our first fight was, and I can't tell you what our last one was, but there have been some doozies in between. What I'm talking about right here, though, is your first big marriage fight. Sure, you had fights before you were married, maybe even on the day of the wedding about her stupid fucking drunk brother losing his glass eye, *again*. How hard is it to re-member where to keep it? This time, though, you two are mar-ried, and your first married fight is different. It's the first indication that marriages, like everything else, are vulnerable. It has an unexpected weight that hits you harder than you antici-pated.

It's crucial to remember that both of you had different experi-ences growing up: different households, parents, rituals, foods, communication skills, the list goes on. You both were indoctri-nated on different planets, and now it's time to merge those two planets, but you will both use the instruction manuals from your home planet. So basically, there's an element to marriage where you are alien to each other.

My parents did not fight. And if they did, it was rarely in front of us kids, and not in the way sitcom couples on TV fought. They didn't raise their voices or throw things at one another. My mom would occasionally slam a cupboard or fix a hard glare, but that was enough to make her point. That's not to say it was easy living over at our house. My mother could be devastatingly passive-aggressive by throwing out non sequiturs like, *"Well I guess your mom just doesn't get it,"* while my dad stared into space desper-ately trying to avoid conflict. My mother's face and general vibra-tion could not bury all the things she was feeling and not saying.

I'm not a screamer, a thrower, a slammer, or a threatener. My voice is loud, though, so even if I'm not trying to raise my voice it feels like I'm yelling. Amiira will attest to that fact. I can also pout, sulk, interrupt, and relentlessly talk about something until the person I'm upset with will give up entirely. I'm also horrible at masking my feelings. Like my mother, feelings take up resi-dence on my face almost immediately and do not vacate until the problem is solved. I don't care if you don't want to talk about it. I

HOW TO KEEP YOUR MARRIAGE FROM SUCKING

will make you talk about it or at least make you wildly uncomfortable while I try to make you talk about it.

On the good side, I'm over a problem quickly (*Note from Amiira: "100 percent not true"*), and I'm always looking for resolution. (*By that, I mean I want to resolve it quickly while also harboring it for a lifetime.*) I never think the relationship is over, no matter how heated the argument is. If I'm wrong (which is a lot), I usually come around to it. I'm quick to apologize, and I genuinely want there to be harmony. I am, by nature, a people pleaser, and I want my people pleased.

Amiira is...the opposite. That's all I need to say about that!

(*Hi, Amiira here. Greg is totally right about me being the opposite. I don't want to talk about it for a very long time. I want to think about it, silently seethe, hate your guts, process an irrational anger both viscerally and mentally, so then I can access my actual right-size emotions about it. Then I want to think about it some more. I don't want to talk to you or maybe even look at you until I'm ready, which may be an uncomfortably long time. [Note from Greg: This can mean years.] I just want to avoid you until I've processed my anger, hurt, or whatever thing has tipped me from my axis of happiness. Is that too much to ask? Apparently, yes. Forcing me to talk about things before I'm ready usually leads to me being kind of, if not totally, cunty and mean. If given the proper amount of time to process my way, I'm tremendously rational and forgiving. If given the choice to let me process my way or force me to talk before I'm ready, Greg always chooses wrong. That's okay. We're only nineteen years into our relationship, so it's a learning curve.*)

So, anyway, there you are, in your kitchen, the new car lot, the grocery store—wherever—and you realize you have a *not* so inconsequential difference of opinion. Or one of you, you realize, is exactly how you said you'd be and your partner didn't believe you.

(My friend Paul Gilmartin says, "I couldn't recognize a red flag at a parade." I feel like that some days.) Something has just come up that puts you into a figurative game of chicken because your person won't change like you expected them to. Those are usually the seeds for the first fight.

The first fight is an awakening of sorts. *"Oh, fuck IS this the person I married?"* Suddenly he's not that funny, cleverly dressed, entertaining, thoughtful man you loved, but rather that consistently forgetful, narcissistic dope, whose main thoughts always return to his own well-being above others. And how can he be buying a car, and he doesn't have his driver's license?!

The car dealership fight was real. To preface, I'm the one who will lose his passport halfway around the world two days before coming home from a tour. Or have to cancel his lost credit cards at least nine times a year. Or never lock his front door. Or lose his keys. Any time someone gives me something important to hold onto I want to say, "Why don't we go throw it in the ocean now and be done with it?"

Amiira was really frustrated because we were looking for a truck for me, and I had left my wallet—with my license and credit cards—at home. My argument was that we were a team now, and what difference did it make when it was "our" money anyway? But it was the beginning of a pattern. A man brings his wallet to a car dealership. An adult brings his wallet to a car dealership. I was embarrassed and defensive and tried to hold my ground. The fight didn't last long, and I apologized more than once on the way home. However, the look on Amiira's face as we sat in the dealer's office while I patted down my pockets was so indelible that I wear a chain wallet to this day, and not as some sort of rockabilly throwback, but as a serious attempt to stay married. She realized that she married the guy who is often going to be unprepared, even for the plans he made himself, and she was bummed both at me and herself because there we were.

Sometimes, when married men and women tell stories about their partners, the women seem to come off like naggy fishwives, and the men come off like prehistoric man babies. Fights push us to the black-and-white of a situation and where you are not describing the person but rather the way you felt about them in the moment. Comedians do this all the time effectively. It's funny because it's true, not it's funny because it's funny. Half the time you meet people's spouses and are almost shocked that they are lovely, not the horrible, judgy, monster humans they sounded like in the retelling of a fight. To be clear, Amiira is a brilliant, stylish, elegant lady with an almost regal sense of family and is possessed with the kind of loyalty and grit that make her the "go to" person in a time of crisis. Furthermore, no one has ever loved me more than she has loved me, for she has loved me when she hated me. Has she faults? Sure, that's why we are writing this book.

Here are some key ingredients that go into a "good fight."

1. There was a right and a wrong.
2. There was an understanding of why wrong was wrong.
3. There was more than an apology. There was a solution that resulted in an action.

Fortunately, that's one we are able to laugh about now.

But fights aren't always this cut-and-dry. Some fights are less clear, where you don't understand why you're fighting or genuinely don't think you've done anything wrong. There will be fights that take years for you to understand why you were having it in the first place. There will be silly hurt feeling fights and fights that boil up.

Of the fights we've had, 90 percent of them have been about important things: how we raise our kids, how we treat one another, how we take care of ourselves, the best way to manage the business of this family. Rarely is there a personal attack. Never has there been physical or mental abuse, and there's been loud shouting only a handful of times.

(Amiira here. Look, it's okay to fight. It's how we learn to navigate each other and ourselves as part of a team. Just because you are with a person doesn't mean you are that person or that they are you. Remaining open and teachable is key to any kind of success, and recognizing that you are both still in process, still evolving, and still reactive to your environments is imperative to finding tolerance and forgiveness in your disagreements. You are learning to be a team, and fights are where we learn so much—knowledge, empathy, and the opportunity for growth.

Marriage rips things apart and sews them back together to make them stronger over and over again. You will have a first fight, and it will feel awful. It will hurt way more than your second, sixth, or forty-ninth fight because it's the first one, and you had a perfect streak going. The silver lining is that you learn how to communicate with each other a little better, you get a better sense of triggers, and there's usually some seriously banging make-up sex to be had. Focus on the silver linings; they are the gift that keep you from harboring the negative feelings from that fight. Those fuckers will fester away in the depths of your smallest self only to be brought up at a later date in a new fight where you lord old history and behavior over your spouse to amplify your anger or injury.

Part of learning how to be together is learning how to fight better so your relationship is not damaged beyond repair. If you explain your anger rather than just express it, you're more likely to find yourself seeking solutions together instead of having an argu-

ment. Your tone is just as important as your words. It's two versus the problem, not you against them. You will get through that first fight, and you will get through that twenty-seventh, just as long as that's not on the same day.)

FIGHTERS FORTUNE COOKIE

If you tell someone you're taking the high road,
you're not taking the high road.

• • • •

HOW TO FIGHT

If you'd rather have bad, hard times with your person than good, easy times with someone else, then you have to learn how to fight well with each other. Fighting well is a hard-earned and even harder-kept skill that is among the most difficult parts of being a human. Historically, you've probably had fights that have ended relationships, friendships, or jobs. When you're married, though, you have to live with this person on a daily basis forever, so if you or your spouse is a dirty fighter, your fights will leave scars that never fully heal. Mark our words. You can't unsay something, you can't unhear something, and you can't unfeel something. Once you let hurtful words fly you may cause an injury that no apology can fully heal. Even in a heated moment when you want to lash out and hurt your person, you have to do your utmost to temper that impulse.

We all want to be bigger than we are during a big fight. Personally, we both have said some super shitty things to each other in the heat of the moment that we still regret and/or are still hold-ing on to as evidence of what the other's true feelings really are. You can't hit delete and rewrite those bullets that come firing out of your mouth. Therefore, it's imperative to set some ground rules for fighting in your marriage early in the newlywed season. There are rules that you should always try to abide by in a fight with anyone, but especially your spouse. If at all possible, start with taking your personal pre-fight inventory. This quick process will help diffuse some of your energy and let you see things a little clearer by engaging your head in the situation while your feelings are all worked up.

Pre-Fight Inventory

1. Why am I upset?
2. What is the real reason?
3. Am I just upset about this one specific thing, or am I bun-dling bigger feelings and using this new event to support or justify my anger?
4. Is this problem a bigger thing that we need to unpack?
5. Can I express my feelings with words and tones without getting too heated, amplified, condescending, or hurtful?
6. Can I attempt to come to a compromise that will make me feel better? Will an apology make a difference, or am I just looking to be right and lash out?
7. Will this matter to me a week from now?
8. Will this matter to me a month from now?
9. Will this matter to me a year from now?
10. What is the real size of this issue? What is comparable and not comparable?

Once you know what size your problem is and whether it is really the issue, and after you strip away the flood of angry energy, you can engage in what will hopefully be a productive fight with respect and love. We made our own Fight Club rules. We don't always stick to them, but, if you can remember some of them in the moment, they can save you some real pain and agony.

Fight Club Rules

1. Don't start a fight right before one of you has to leave to be somewhere at a certain time. (BTW, this is harder than it sounds.)
2. No name calling (unless it's sweetheart, sugar tush, honey schnookums, etc.).
3. No interrupting when the other person is talking (we know—impossible—but try anyway).
4. No blaming or accusations (even if the other person is to blame and is clearly at fault).
5. No cussing (Amiira never can manage this one).
6. No yelling (this escalates things too quickly and amplifies the fear level but surprisingly does nothing to make you more heard).
7. No sarcasm (again, Amiira cannot even manage this for a minute).
8. No defensiveness (getting defensive reads the same as saying I'm only concerned with being right, not hearing you out).
9. No generalizations. (*"You always are a fucking nightmare, and you never remember to not be an asshole."*)
10. No physical or emotional gestures, intimidation, threats, or violence.

11. No walking out without setting up a time to continue. (Go blow off some steam, but first be decent enough to acknowledge that you will make resolving your issues a priority after you've cooled down.)

12. It's okay to go to bed mad and wake up mad. (But it's hard to be mad at someone who brings you the first cup of coffee. Just saying that coffee has powers of transcendence.)

• • • •

EVERYONE JUST WANTS TO FEEL SAFE (A GUIDED MEDITATION)

It occurred as we wrote this that 95 percent of all fights are about the same thing. People want to be heard. You are more than likely fighting because you are doing something your person has asked you not to do or has asked you one hundred thousand times *to* do, or they really need help doing. Before you craft your response, stop. Close your eyes. Take a deep deep breath, in through the nose, out through the mouth. Think about what your person is asking you to do, or to never do again, or again accusing you of doing.

Let's walk through why this is upsetting for them. Imagine what it is about your transgression that makes your partner feel unsafe. Now realize that is what's going on. They are scared. It may sound like they hate you for never understanding that when you take your underpants off, the underpants don't then walk themselves into the washing machine. They are scared of not being seen, of not being enough, of not getting what they want. Whatever it is. Even if you are not to blame.

Think to yourself, "How can I help? How can I make the person who I love so much feel safe?" Then, when you are ready, open your eyes...your partner should be gone. Well fuck, of course they're gone! They brought up something important, and you just closed your eyes and sat there with your mouth open. You idiot! Go find them and ask how you can help.

14

sex-pectations versus sex-pectreality

IN THE BEGINNING OF marriage there is sex—a lot of hot, hot sex. The first five are the Golden Sex Years (unless you have a baby, but more on that later). Sex is not only fun and exciting but it's also a temporary solution to all problems and questions. What's for dinner? Sex. How are we going to pay rent this month? Sex. Are you mad at me? Sex. What do you want for your birthday? Sex. How many fingers am I holding up? Sex. You're both up for it all the time. All plans end with sex or the promise of sex happening soon.

When you're falling in love and getting it on, you are quite sure that the sex you're having can't be topped...until the next time you have sex. The anticipation, the build-up of sexual tension, coupled with the newness of your relationship is like a perfect storm of sex nirvana.

When you become engaged, the sex gets even better because you're becoming official, and that's even hotter. Sex is as amazing and frequent as *50 Shades of Grey* or *Deadpool* would have you believe when you're newly engaged and madly in love. Then you get married and you have hot newlywed sex, which is also incredibly, surprisingly, hot. Surprising not only because you didn't think it possible but even more so because everyone—yes, everyone—projects what a bummer married sex life is like. We've all been exposed to it in some, if not many, forms, so there's a subconscious fear already implanted that your sex life will go into the shitter. You just don't know *when* it's going in the shitter.

You start thinking that maybe you and your spouse are the exception to the rule because your super-hot newlywed sex is totally surpassing what married sex, even at the beginning, is supposed to be like, according to all known evidence and references. You should probably congratulate yourselves then write your own self-help married sex how-to book and become sex gurus. We hope you're right, and you are the exception, by the way. Also, we are looking forward to hearing more about what life is like in the perfect utopian dimension you and your spouse have ascended to. Does Amazon Prime deliver with drones there? Are there spacesuits and jetpacks like we were promised?

In the first five years, sex still brings you closer together. It is the glue, it's still the priority. Once you're past the five-year mark, sex isn't the headliner on the bill anymore. Sex has been knocked down the ladder by kids, jobs, fatigue, Netflix, eating too much, feeling bloated, so on and so forth. You reach an understanding where you can be honest with each other about what you would rather do than have sex at any given moment. Time passes, as does the newness of your sex life. Together you continue to evolve in your marriage, and things take on an expanded form. The intimacy becomes the language you speak in your common life together rather than being defined by the sex you have. Sex can still be awesome, don't get us wrong, *it just is no longer the glue.*

Learning to be intimate without sex is a major step in deepening the connection of your relationship, which is landmark stuff. So that will be great and very meaningful…but honestly it is not as exciting as new, hot sex. This is often when one person in the relationship gets the nagging feeling that there's something wrong with their sex life. The first five set a high watermark that is seared into your consciousness, against which you measure your sex life for the rest of time. It's a blessing and a curse.

• • • •

THE ROUTINE OF ROUTINES

Here's something to chew on. Even if you don't plan on having kids, or buying a house, or any of the common tropes that come with marriage, you are, in fact, settling down. Settling down in no way implies inactive or without purpose. What it means is that you are at the beginning of setting up routines. There is nothing wrong with routines. They are what comfort us. They are there to establish whatever your version of normalcy may be. They are setting up a home base, nesting, or whatever you want to call it. It's one of the great joys of being married. Most people who get married seem, in some way, to be looking for this. We were.

Both settling and routine are hard words to reckon with. At the beginning, it won't even feel like that is what's happening, even though it actually is. You will have more sex, see more movies, go to more restaurants, have more parties, and spend more time with friends. But this won't last forever. Please don't put that expectation on yourselves as a couple. At some point, maybe even early in your newlywed-dom, you will also probably have less sex. Think about it like exercise. Sometimes you're really into it and work out four times a week for a few months in a row. You're slay-

ing it, and it feels great to do something great for your mind, body, and health. Then shit comes up, and you don't hit a gym or a class for six weeks. You just cannot make it happen for whatever reason. It's okay. Truly. Your slaying days will come back around, as will the days you can't seem to get lift off.

Don't listen to the harmful magazine articles that position themselves as marriage self-help but really only serve to cast doubt on the uniqueness of your marriage. No one knows you two and what makes you happy better than you do.

When we first got married, date nights were a trendy concept. The idea being that you have to actually schedule time in to honor your relationship as a couple. It's not a horrible idea, but the undertone brings up the notion that the comfort you have in the relationship to just hang at home isn't enough. That not having dates could mean things are going south in your marriage, or that you've begun to take each other for granted. There is a great value in making sure you spend quality time with your significant other, you'll get no argument on that one. But just because you don't go out on date nights doesn't mean you are doing anything wrong. We, of course, took the bait that we might be messing up our marriage, so we had at a "date night." It was fun, it was fine, but you know what? It lasted about an hour and a half before we both admitted that we just wanted to go home to be together there. That is where we are happiest, which actually is a gigantic victory.

There's also a lot written about the implications of not having enough sex that it somehow will end your marriage. This never stops being a hot magazine topic or clickbait on the internet. When you're a newlywed, you will have a booming sex life. Indulge and enjoy, but know that there will be an ebb and flow to

your sex life, and often it starts to establish itself when you're newlyweds. As you settle into your routines together, you'll find that sometimes one of you would rather watch a show or read a book than get it on. There will be people and articles and movies that make you think you should panic. Don't panic. Your sex life is good if it feels good to both of you. Simple as that. There is no race or magic number you are supposed to beat in your newlywed state. As you get older, regardless of the state of your marriage and sex life, you will choose a nap over sex at least half (if not all) the time the choice is offered. You will choose catching up on *Game of Thrones* over having sex. You will choose getting to complete a conversation with your spouse over having sex. Know why? Because those things make you happy, too. Because your life gets busy and your responsibilities grow exponentially after your newlywed years. Real intimacy has very little to do with sex and numbers. Real intimacy is about connection, vulnerability, and truth. Great sex is a benefit of great intimacy, not the other way around. Boom! Dropped the mic on that one.

• • • •

SEX TRUTHS

Experts in the field of sexual health and behavior know that sex is not just sex for pleasure most of the time. Subconsciously most of us have figured that out, though it may not have fully entered our real consciousness. If you think about when and why you have sex, the answers vary from love, lust, and connection to motivations less attached to our emotional state than our mental one like power, control, and curiosity. In a marriage, sex is like a Swiss army knife, a tool for every occasion!

Sex is a Reward

Sex is a reward. Sex is a reward for being thoughtful, for being successful, for being hot. Sex is a reward for saying or doing the right thing at the right time. Sex is a reward for being drunk. Sex is a reward for instilling a feeling of safety, for installing safety features in your home. Sex is a reward for loyalty, for making you feel beautiful, or seen, or wanted, for picking your person over someone else in any given situation. Sex is a reward for a job well done, or one done not so well but done nevertheless. Sex is a reward for good behavior of all kinds, for remembering to do something. Sex is a reward for not letting you down. Sex is a reward for nearly any situation that is deemed reward-worthy to the giver of the sex.

Don't be naïve, and don't pretend it's not the truth. Don't pretend like you've never rewarded your special someone with sex, either. Acknowledging that sex is a reward doesn't diminish anything about it; it just illuminates how the reward system evolves as your marriage evolves. In the early days, you looked for reasons to reward each other with sex. Sex rewards were given liberally at the beginning of the marriage because you were still in the new version of you as a couple. The version where you were always thoughtful of each other and deeply connected in your own symbiotic synchronicity. You didn't have to work that hard for it, and you'd do it even if you were honestly too tired. And with real-life responsibilities at a minimum—far smaller than later in marriage—not much cuts into your sex time. So, the reward of sex gets handed out often.

Ask any couple married more than fifteen years and they will tell you that being rewarded with sex is a much rarer occurrence. There are times when getting rewarded with sex will seem like a mirage far in the distance. Something unreachable and not even real. Not for any other reason than there is just too much of your life together clouding up and getting in the way of rewarding your person with sex. However, for the person used to being rewarded frequently with sex, it will feel like they have to metaphorically rescue a baby from a house fire to get laid.

The flip side of sex being a reward is *withholding* sex as a punishment. Oh, it happens. However, because sex is a reward, there can easily be the illusion that sex is being withheld when it's not. Sometimes you just don't have the time to reward your person with some hot sex because you have to be at the office, the kids have to be picked up from practice, you have your period, and you're totally fucking miserable and don't want anything other than a glass of wine and a Midol.

Sex is a Band-Aid

Sex is a Band-Aid. Sex is a Band-Aid for being sad, for being lonely, for being selfish or busy. Sex is a Band-Aid to cover a small wound or indiscretion. Sex is a Band-Aid for a fight, for a wounded ego, to cover an excuse. Sex is a Band-Aid for depression. Sex is a Band-Aid for low self-esteem, for need. Sex is the thing you put on the situation to buy time until the intensity passes. Sex is a Band-Aid that makes things better, for now. Sex is good medicine, a temporary cure that takes the sting out and gives you a whole different set of the feels. Sometimes you just need to feel differently than you do, and sex can pull you right out of whatever funk or fucked feeling you might be sinking into. Sex isn't a long-term fix or solution, but that doesn't stop people from testing that theory or wanting it to be.

Sex is a Motivator

Sex is a motivator. The things that people find sexy manifest into action. If someone thinks they will get to have more hot sex, they will do almost anything. Be more ambitious, work out more, help you move, drive you to the airport, babysit your nephew, dog sit your elderly dog with incontinent bowels, dress different, be different, be whoever they need to be to get laid. It's the God's honest truth. Want something done quickly? Offer sex. That shit will get done quick. Men by nature are sexually driven, so their desire for sex is a relative constant, and that can be exploited for good in a marriage. Your husband likely won't mind that you are offering to give him sex in exchange for whatever it is that needs doing. It doesn't work as well in reverse, as women can generally get sex when they want it from their spouses. Sorry, fellas.

• • • •

FUTURE SEX LIFE CRYSTAL BALL

We all know the tropes about married sex being boring and infrequent. Truth is, these are tropes because there is some truth in it.

Don't panic.

That doesn't mean that your sex life will suck, but it most definitely will change as the years pass. Like anything that was once new, you will eventually fall into a rhythm of familiarity with your married sex. You may get lazy about tending to it, and you choose other Sunday pastimes over it as you get more comfortable together or more tired. When you have kids and don't have sleep, sleep will win over a quickie nine times out of ten. No guilt there. It's possible you won't even notice that you've been having less sex until suddenly you notice that you're having less sex.

You will wonder if there's a problem in your marriage, if you need to do something to spice it up, or if you're the only one noticing. There will be periods where all you want to do is figure out when you're having sex next and periods when you willfully avoid having to have it. It's normal to go in and out of sexual phases in your long-term relationship. Not everyone is having a better sex life than you, so don't fret.

Sometimes sex doesn't fit into your week or even month unless you schedule it. We've been together nearly twenty years and have gone through dry spells that required scheduled sex to finally be broken. With two kids, three dogs, a house, work commitments out of town, and different bedtimes, there are so many moving pieces to our daily life. We are rarely both available, awake, and/or game for sex at the same time. The interest level is still there, but there aren't enough hours in the day where we are kid-free and unencumbered. Your life will continue to get more complex, and your free time will continue to evaporate as your life together evolves and gets richer.

So how do you Keep your Sex Life from Sucking? To start, don't put unrealistic expectations on each other. Get real about what may come down the pike for you, and remember that you are in this together. The person you married is your favorite person in the world, and the only person you'll have sex with until death do you part. Keeping your sex life exciting, interesting, vibrant, and fulfilling is a challenge, but it's one worth taking on.

THE TWO SIDES OF THE COIN

the upside of not having as much sex as you used to...

When you do have it, it will rock your world and remind you how great your sex is. Then you will make plans to have sex more often because your mind-blowing sex will reinforce that, even if you don't have it a lot, when you do have it it's epic.

the downside of not having as much sex as you used to...

You're so agitated about not having enough sex that you put too much pressure on yourself and your spouse to have it. Then, when you do have it, you are so fixated with getting it done that you don't fully enjoy it.

the upside of scheduling sex...

You actually know when you're having sex, so you can groom and prep appropriately so there's fresh breath, tidy pubes, and sexy underwear. Everyone appreciates when their partner smells good and has made an event out of having sex.

the downside of scheduling sex...

The lack of spontaneity really makes you feel like an old married couple, which is comparable to a punch to the kidneys... and, yet, you're still getting to have sex, so you should really stop complaining, and be thankful that your spouse still wants to have sex with you.

15

glory and struggle

ARRIAGE IS AT BEST a preposterous idea. It is an antiquated institution that is slower at catching up with modern times than civil rights. It makes you place impossible expectations and unspoken limitations upon the only person who's ever really let you in on the real you. AND it starts off with a celebration that has all the hubris of getting the Vince Lombardi trophy before you've played Super Bowl. Marriage is simultaneously both hard and glorious. When you're newlyweds, you get much more glorious than hard, but the balance will shift and morph continually as you and your life together evolves. Newlywed-dom is a comet that passes through the night sky only once, and it is so truly special. It's when you fall deeper in love with your spouse than you even thought possible. It's when your life is filled with possibility and hope above all else. It's when you become deeply rooted to each other and intertwined to a new degree. It's magic. But, like magic, it disappears. Not the happiness or the love, but the simplicity that newlywed life has to offer. Life and marriage aren't always simple, so appreciate the gift that these first years are in your life.

THE TWO SIDES OF THE COIN

the upside of doing it right...

You will create an incredible foundation for the years to come based on love and respect that will inform how you treat each other, how you address challenges together, and how you sustain a thriving marriage.

the downside of doing it right...

You've created a blueprint for a healthy marriage that is the envy of all of your friends who now hate your guts because being around you only highlights the crap in their relationship that isn't working. Now you have to go and find new friends.

the upside of doing it wrong...

You can always say you didn't know what the hell you were doing and not play dumb, for once.

the downside of doing it wrong...

You have no one to blame but yourselves...and reality television for making hyper-drama seem normal and worthy of replicating. And, also, divorce is expensive.

MARRIAGE FORTUNE COOKIE

Keep the sexy and the mystery alive, always close the bathroom door when it's "go time."

• • • •

THE BEST NEWLYWED STORY
OF ANYONE WE KNOW

We only met Jim and Steph a few times, but they absolutely fascinate us. In their first year of marriage, they decided that they wanted to go on the adventure of a lifetime together before they settled down. They didn't want to spend their lives behind a desk then wake up one day and realize that they didn't really live while they had the chance. It took them two years of working to save enough money for what they had planned, but once they did, they took off.

Jim and Steph sold almost everything they owned and bought a sailboat. They mapped a course to sail around the world. For seven years they literally sailed the seas, anchored in amazing locales, and lived off of the land (and sea) much of the time. They built huts on uninhabited islands and made friends with animals. They learned to fish, ate the fruit from the trees, and slept in hammocks under the stars, or just drifted in the ocean for weeks at a time just being together alone in the sea.

They even had two babies during their time sailing around the world. When it became time for their children to go to school, Jim and Steph decided to settle down in Hawaii. The ocean was such a huge part of their life that they needed to be near it always. When they showed us some home movies of their newlywed years, they looked so free, in love, and blissfully happy. Their story is so unlike anyone else's and so inspiring. For seven years, they had nothing but each other (by choice, mind you), and it was all they needed.

• • • •

THE WORST NEWLYWED STORY
OF ANYONE WE KNOW

Our friend, Gwyn, married her boyfriend of seven years, James. They had been together long enough to already seem married. They had merged their lives years ago, lived together, and had a dog. Their extended families even went on full family vacations together. Getting married shouldn't have changed much of anything for this couple.

During their first newlywed year, Gwyn noticed that James was at times acting like a different person. He would get really angry about seemingly inconsequential things or get super depressed and down. His sense of humor was particularly ribald, and he made Gwyn nervous at times by the way he looked at her. She was really worried about him, and we were really worried about her. Every time we saw Gwyn, she looked worn out and was getting thinner and thinner. She said that James was so mercurial that she felt like she had married a stranger. James's parents were concerned, as well, but James shut them out.

About sixteen months into their marriage, Gwyn and James started seeing a couples' therapist. The therapist finally pried out the information that James, who was bipolar and manic depressive (which Gwyn was aware of), had stopped taking his medication right after their honeymoon (which she was totally unaware of). James decided that he wanted to experience his life without medication and had no intention of going back to being on meds. His mood swings were frightening, and Gwyn soon found herself avoiding going home.

Gwyn tried reasoning with James, but he wouldn't listen. She tried begging him, but he didn't care. She didn't know what to do.

In a therapy session, he revealed that he didn't actually want to have children anymore and that he was quitting his job. Gwyn had invested most of her twenties in this relationship, had planned her future with James, and their life together was being completely disregarded. Gwyn and James separated for a year and almost called it quits before their second anniversary.

James ultimately reached the conclusion that his mental illness was something that he needed to treat and respect, as was his marriage to Gwyn. They made it through—barely—but they not only missed out on the great newlywed bliss period but are still regaining their balance and trying to heal from the trauma of those first two years.

• • • •

WHEN IT STARTS OUT WORSE (BECAUSE SOMETIMES IT DOES)

Greg here. Look, Amiira and I are not blind optimists, nor are we fools. To almost every semi-certainty we posit in this book, we know there is an opposite way of seeing it. There will be an exception to a rule. We are taking the sum total of our collective experience with an institution we believe in that has served not only us but our families, as well. We have been through our fair share of worse. Probably no more than any other folks who have been married more than a minute, but enough where the possibility—even the plausibility—of calling it off was in no way off the table. Gratefully, neither of us ever wanted to call it off at the same time. There was always one of us willing to fight to right the ship and pull the other one back to shore. The point I want to make is that most married couples will tell you that you have to bleed for it a little. Over the years you will lose a little dignity, faith, stature, money, health, and family along the way, but that's all a part of the WORSE in the legendary phrase "for better or for worse."

But what happens when it starts out worse? What happens during this newlywed phase when things are supposed to be mostly great but it's absolutely not? Here's the truth and hopefully it's not your truth, but if it is, better to be prepared for it: Sometimes it's just not going to work. Most likely, it wasn't working before you got married, but that didn't stop you from getting married. Many use marriage as a way of solving a relationship problem, thinking that committing to marriage will put an umbrella over a leaky relationship—even very smart, intuitive people make that mistake. Or maybe you didn't have all the conversations one needs to have before getting married. Maybe someone decided to stop taking their medication and has turned into someone you don't even recognize. Maybe you were just wrong—or possibly drunk.

There's never shame in choosing the life that's best for you. If the "for worse" in the "for better and for worse" is all you seem to be getting at the beginning, you're allowed to call a timeout to save yourself. We give you permission, your family and friends will give you permission, and you have to give yourself permission. We know you probably didn't enter into marriage lightly and don't want to give up on it quickly. We don't want you to either. So, if your newlywed marriage is a suckfest, seek couples' therapy, individual therapy, and then the counsel of your friends, your loved ones, your church, your spirit animal, and, ultimately, your gut. It takes two to make it work and be willing to do the work to make it work. But if that's not the case, it can't be fixed, and it's better that you realize that now and not ten years from now.

• • • •

THE STRUGGLE

How To Keep Your Marriage from Sucking is meant for those in the early years of what we hope will become a very long marriage. Our companion book, *We Used To Be In Love, Now We Just Work Here,* will follow and deal with the more intense hardships that marriages face. We wanted to address the *"for worse,"* both little and soul crushing, in the "for better or for worse" that you signed up for separately as this book is meant to be more about awareness and prevention rather than crisis.

That being said, one of the biggest issues that plagues marriages and leads to many of the aforementioned *"for worses"* is the habit we have to remember to not "glorify" the bad stuff much more than we do the good stuff. It takes five positives to diffuse one negative. The negatives scream with a much higher volume than positives, which is such a testament to how screwed up we are as human beings. It's the same principle of getting a thousand positive reviews and one negative where the negative one becomes the only one that matters. Or the concept that it takes many good deeds to build a good reputation and only one bad deed to ruin one. Yes, we know, this is totally fucked, but the same goes for relationship math. The good/bad ratio is unfortunately very real and often the undoing of a once healthy marriage.

The trespasses and historic slights or injuries between two people take up a bigger space than their *"acts of love"* counterparts. Sometimes we don't even clock the acts of love that we are getting from our partner. We assume the acts of love are part of the spousal job description and therefore doesn't warrant actual credit or acknowledgement. And BOOM!! That's how it starts. We notice the bad and not the good. We scold the bad and don't reward the good. We remember the bad and forget the good. It's a recipe for disaster and resentment. Unless you decide to be different. Marriage is not a status, it's a practice. You can choose to practice in a space of gratitude and forgiveness rather than scorekeeping. The marriage struggle is as real as you allow it to be. Don't be a passenger on the bumpy road to Suckville. Be the one that sets the destination to glory and pilots yourself there with the grace your life deserves.

• • • •

THE SOLUTION IS IN THE SET-UP

An exceptional marriage requires an exceptional set-up. That's the truth, but it's a truth that you can be an active participant in or ignore completely. Being diligently mindful is the way to not only honor your marriage but to safeguard it from harm. We all plant seeds in our relationship that can sprout into flowers or weeds depending on which ones we water, so choose wisely. Seeds can sprout into resentments when someone feels repeatedly unheard, unconsidered, or dismissed. These little transgressions are often at the root of bigger injury and trauma to a marriage. What you do with these injuries and resentments is a choice. They can grow into something unwieldy or be diffused through thoughtful communication, positive action, and active forgiveness. We repeat what we don't repair. If you want to have a suck-free marriage, it requires working through the hiccups and hurt to rid yourself of their stain *when they happen*. Holding on to the negative is the fastest way to grow the weeds of marital damage.

The practice, not the goal, is to learn how to love each other even when you struggle to like each other. To recognize that keeping your marriage from sucking isn't about marrying the right partner, it's about being the right partner. Understanding that there is no winner and loser in a marriage. You either win together or lose together. The answer to "How do you keep your marriage from sucking?" is also the key to having a happy marriage. It's a combination of intention and letting go. Set your intention to be mindful, loving, and forgiving partners, and let go of the things that don't serve your marriage.

It's taken us a very long time to not only realize this but to be able to live like this. Hurt people hurt people. It's very easy to be hurt by the person you love the most in the world. Minimizing the hurt you inflict on your partner, unintentionally or not, is an act of love that will reward you in longevity. Championing the friendship, support, and devotion to each other will result in an intimacy that saves you in the bleakest of times. Your marriage doesn't have to be a hell ride or a prison. It gets to be a sanctuary and a privilege. Whatever you focus on you will experience. That's the law we just made up so we're pretty sure it's true. You got this. Now go and be awesome.

Love,

Amiira & Greg

acknowledgments

THE AUTHORS would like to acknowledge:

That they are not professional therapists or counselors, just lifelong behavior and relationship enthusiasts. We have nothing but respect and admiration for those who pursued those professions and we encourage all individuals and couples to seek professional counsel when needed and even when not needed. Therapy turns walls into windows.

Our agent, Kerry Sparks, without whose endless patience, support, and understanding this book would not exist. Kerry stuck with us through many years and incarnations as did her team at Levine/Greenberg/Rostan, especially Daniel Greenberg and Elizabeth Fisher. Thank you, thank you, thank you.

Our publisher, Keith Wallman, at Diversion Books who is a dream collaborator disguised as an everyday gentleman. Thank you for getting us, our vision for this book, the next book, and helping us shape them both. Thank you to the Diversion team, specifically Scott Waxman, Sarah Masterson Hally, and Alexandra Israel. Additional thank you to those who helped over the lifespan of writing this book: Kathryn

Cardoso, Jaime Levine, Mary Cummings, and Randall Klein.

Our brilliant creative friends, Chris Bilheimer, art designer extraordinaire, for always creating the perfect book covers for us, and Anthony Dalesandro for having the kind of photographic eye and skill to make us look much more attractive than we are in real life.

Our families whose encouragement and faith is unparalleled. Sharon and Bill Ruotola, Curt and Christine Ruotola, Shelley Coscina, Koke'e Coscina, Gina Coscina, Dick Behrendt, Ricki Pollycove, Kristen Behrendt. Thank you for always having our backs and believing.

Our incredible children, True and Mighty, who are and will always be *everything* to us. You are the true reason we were brought together in this lifetime and it is an honor to be your parents. Truly.

Amiira: Thank you to my dear friends who helped nudge me forward at the most vital moments sharing their own wisdom, experiences, and laughter. This book would have never been finished without the cheerleading, hand holding, and devotion of Christine Taylor, Jackie Harris, Paul Greenberg, Lauren Levine, Moon Zappa, Vivianne Fernquist, Heidi Herzon, Alli Shearmur, Lisa Dalesandro, Lindsay Chelsom, Andrea Frank, Tracey Cooperstein, and Valerie Azlynn. Each one of you put your arms around me and helped me to cross the finish line when it seemed unfathomable. I am lucky beyond measure to be so loved by you brilliant, hilarious humans. Thank you to my parents, Bill and Sharon, who showed me what a marriage can be and what love looks like.

Greg: I would like to thank my father for showing me there's no age at which a man cannot continue to grow. Three new friends who shouted "Just fucking write the book": Sam Scott, Cheryl Espisito, and John Henson. Kay Hanley and Michael Eisenstein, of whom I always say, "The best married couple I know is divorced." My beleaguered manager, Jakob Markowitz, and finally, Moon Zappa, who has been our marriage Sherpa through good and bad, and who led us to podcasting, which is why you are now holding this book in your hand. Last but never least, my many tireless fans across all mediums who patiently wait for me to figure it out.

Each other for never giving up on us as we weathered the trials and tribulations that inform this book.

about the authors

Greg Behrendt is a comedian and author. Co-author of the *New York Times* bestselling book *He's Just Not That Into You*, which was adapted into a major motion picture, he was also a script consultant to the series *Sex and the City*. Greg currently spends time parenting, touring as a standup, and recording his podcast *Rock Out with Your Doc Out* with Kay Hanley. He someday hopes to lie down.

Amiira Ruotola took to writing after retiring from a tremendously adventurous career in the music business at a young age with little hearing left to speak of. She has sold scripts to FOX, CBS, and NBC, and is currently developing a show for YouTube Red. In addition to working in the relationship field, Amiira is writing her first novel. She cannot keep fish alive and may or may not have been raised by spies.

Together, Amiira and Greg have written *It's Called A Breakup Because It's Broken* and *It's Just A F***ing Date*. They appeared with Oprah Winfrey for an *Oprah's Lifeclass* based on their work, and they now host the podcast *Maybe It's You*. They live in Los Angeles, raising their two ridiculously incredible children and three dogs.